Contents

Abstract

A brief introduction to the Curculionoidea is given. The biology, life history and phenology, and economic importance of orthocerous weevils is discussed, and methods of collecting, preservation, examination and dissection described. The adult characteristics of the group, which includes the Nemonychidae, Urodontidae, Anthribidae, Attelabidae and Apionidae, are outlined. The use of the keys is explained. A summary of hostplant records and a check list of species are provided.

Illustrated keys are given to the families of Curculionoidea and to genera and species within families and subfamilies of the orthocerous group. The entry for each species includes information on biology and larval hostplants, a brief summary of distribution in the British Isles, and an outline of the zoogeographic range.

Weevils (superfamily Curculionoidea): general introduction

The group of families centred on, and including, the Curculionidae, is a particularly large assemblage of species. Modern taxonomic work has established the superfamily Curculionoidea as the equivalent of the older 'series' Rhynchophora. The group Curculionoidea has been relatively stable taxonomically, with only the Bruchidae as a family occasionally placed within it, though more usually included in the Chrysomeloidea. Within the Curculionoidea there has been much less stability. One school, adopting by implication the principle of the conservation of obligatory categories, has retained the family Curculionidae to include various groups such as Nemonychinae, Attelabinae and Apioninae as subfamilies, while accepting the traditional view which regards Anthribidae, Scolytidae and Platypodidae as distinct families (Aslam 1961; Dieckmann 1974, 1977; Kissinger 1968). A less conservative view has been put by Crowson (1950–1954 (1967), 1956), Morimoto (1962, 1976) and others, and followed by Kloet & Hincks (1977). These authors accept that there are valid reasons for regarding several curculionid groups as good families. In the British fauna these families are the Nemonychidae, Attelabidae and Apionidae. To these must be added the Urodontidae (Crowson, 1984), following the recent discovery that *Bruchela rufipes* (Oliv.) is a resident British species. Together with the Anthribidae, these families constitute the 'orthocerous' weevils dealt with in this handbook.

In his key to the families of Coleoptera in this series of handbooks, Crowson (1956) recognised seven families of Curculionoidea. Of these, only the Scolytidae and Platypodidae have so far been keyed to species in these publications (Duffy, 1953). For the identification of other species of weevils, the student has had to use Fowler (1891), Joy (1932), or continental works dealing with faunas larger than the British, such as Hoffmann (1945, 1950, 1954, 1958), Dieckmann (1972, 1974, 1977, 1980) or Freude, Harde & Lohse (1981, 1983), supplemented by the literature. Fowler's great work, though still of considerable interest and importance, is now very much out of date, though improved in part by the later supplementary volume (Fowler & Donisthorpe, 1913). Joy (1932) is difficult to use because it is so abbreviated and relies so heavily on comparative characters. Of the three continental works, Dieckmann's are the most useful, not least in the biological detail given, which demonstrates the progress in this field which has been made since Fowler's day. However, Dieckmann's papers do not as yet cover the whole weevil fauna of East Germany.

The present handbook covers five families (Nemonychidae, Anthribidae, Urodontidae, Attelabidae and Apionidae) of the Curculionoidea, but only 117 species. About 425 species of British weevils remain to be dealt with in the Curculionidae *sensu stricto*.

Handbooks for the
Identification of British Insects

Vol. 5, Part 16

Editors: W. R. Dolling & R. R. Askew

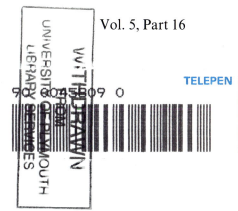
ORTHOCEROUS WEEVILS

A
E,
ND

)

DON

The aim of the *Handbooks* is to provide illustrated identification keys to the insects of Britain, together with concise morphological, biological and distributional information. The series also includes a *Check List of British Insects*.

Each part should serve both as an introduction to a particular group of insects and as an identification manual.

Details of handbooks currently available can be obtained from Publications Sales, The Natural History Museum, Cromwell Road, London SW7 5BD.

World List abbreviation: *Handbk Ident. Br. Insects.*

© Royal Entomological Society of London, 1990

First published 1990 by the British Museum (Natural History) at The Natural History Museum, London.

ISBN 0 901546 69 0

Printed in Great Britain by Henry Ling Ltd., at the Dorset Press, Dorchester, Dorset.

Acknowledgements

Preparation of a handbook such as this must be based on the work of many entomologists past and present. Particular thanks are offered to the Trustees and governing bodies of the British Museum (Natural History), Cambridge University Museum of Zoology, and Manchester Museum, for the loan of specimens and opportunities to study collections in their care. I am also grateful to my own institution, the Institute of Terrestrial Ecology, (NERC), and its former and current Directors, Mr J. N. R. Jeffers, Dr J. P. Dempster and Dr T. M. Roberts for facilities.

The following workers have helped me by lending specimens, or in many other different ways: Mr D. M. Appleton, Dr R. G. Booth, Mr J. Cooter, Drs Sarah A. Corbet, J. P. Dempster, Lothar Dieckmann and E. Duffey, Messrs P. M. Hammond, P. T. Harding and P. J. Hodge, Dr P. S. Hyman, Mr C. Johnson, Prof. D. A. Jones, Dr M. L. Luff, Prof. J. A. Owen, Mr J. A. Parry, Mons. J. Péricart, Mrs M. K. Perkins, Messrs R. Plant, R. D. Pope, R. W. J. Read, and W. E. Rispin, the late Dr J. Smart, Mr R. T. Thompson, Dr R. C. Welch and Dr M. A. Alonso Zarazaga.

I owe a particular debt of gratitude to Mr R. W. John Read for the drawings of whole insects which embellish this handbook.

I thank my wife and family for both encouragement and forbearance.

Orthocerous weevils: families Nemonychidae, Anthribidae, Urodontidae, Attelabidae and Apionidae

Introduction

Except from a structural and taxonomic viewpoint, there is little to distinguish orthocerous weevils from the Curculionidae (the non-orthocerous group). The five families comprising the orthocerous group are disparate in both their biology and their species richness. The Nemonychidae and Urodontidae each have only one British representative, and our 8 species of Anthribidae are all rare or local. Many Attelabidae are both commoner and more conspicuous. Some are relatively large weevils, are brightly coloured, and attract attention by the leaf-rolls constructed on various trees, especially birch, oak and hazel, for the nutrition of their larvae. The most conspicuous orthocerous weevils are the Apionidae. Despite their small size and often sombre colouring, many species are abundant and active, and some are pests. The 84 species of *Apion* which, together with two *Nanophyes* species, comprise the British Apionidae, include over 70% of the orthocerous weevils in Britain.

Like other weevils, most orthocerous species are found on, or in, plants or plant material of various kinds.

Biology

In both adult and larval stages the British Curculionoidea are phytophagous; the only exceptions are the two species of *Anthribus* (= *Brachytarsus*), which feed as larvae on coccids. Nearly all the species considered in this handbook are stenophagous, i.e. they are restricted in their 'choice' and utilisation of food. The degree of restriction varies from oligophagy (feeding on one family of plants) to monophagy (feeding on one genus or species of plant only). Fungi are utilised by a few Anthribidae, and gymnosperms by the Nemonychidae (one British species), but apart from these only angiosperms are attacked. Weevil larvae feed in a wide range of different plant structures, but predominantly in stems, buds and fruits. Leaf-rolling is a specialised kind of behaviour found in several Attelabidae and is an adaptation which makes leaf tissue available as larval food. A list of hostplant records is given on pp. 11–15.

Larval taxonomy is outside the scope of this handbook. The classic work of van Emden (1938, 1952) has provided a foundation for a modern treatise on the taxonomy of European weevil larvae which has been only partially realised by Scherf (1964) and others.

Although the foodplants of most species of stenophagous weevils are broadly known, there is much need of exact and detailed observations and in recent years more progress has been made in this field in continental Europe than in the British Isles. Most weevils are endophagous as larvae, with only a few Curculionidae that are ecto-phagous, although some *Apion* larvae feed in a semi-exposed position. In most cases the egg is inserted into the larval feeding site via a hole made with the aid of the rostrum, which in some species is able to penetrate deeply into plant tissue, for example *Curculio* species which oviposit in acorns, nuts and galls.

Adult weevils normally feed on the foliage of the larval host plants. However, more work is needed to ascertain whether alternative foodplants may not be important at certain stages in the life cycle. Some species may be found away from their usual hosts, particularly in spring, when they may be found apparently feeding on pollen of early flowers, or in autumn, when some *Apion* species, which feed as larvae on herbs, are notoriously prevalent on trees and shrubs.

The importance of larval feeding has tended to overshadow other aspects of weevil biology, except in some notorious pest species. A short summary of aspects of biology which have received attention, especially in the British fauna, is given by Morris (1976b).

Life history and phenology

The usual pattern of life history in the Curculionoidea is of a single annual generation, with the adult the longest-lived stage. Adult weevils emerge in spring from hibernation, which probably involves reproductive diapause in most cases. Mating occurs either then or in the previous autumn. A period of adult feeding is probably necessary to enable the gonads to mature. Eggs are laid in early summer and larvae develop rapidly to emerge as adults in late summer or early autumn. A period of activity, particularly dispersal and adult feeding, often precedes hibernation.

Some species of *Apion* are either known to be, or are suspected of being, double-brooded. However, observations that a species occurs as an adult in, say, May and October, normally mean that there is one annual generation with larvae occurring in June and July, rather than two generations (*cf.* Day, 1915, referring to *Apion genistae*).

The phenology of the structures in which weevil larvae feed can greatly modify the temporal pattern of the occurrence of adults, by effectively accelerating or retarding the post-diapause phase in relation to the calendar year. However, this is more marked in species of the curculionid genera *Anthonomus* and *Dorytomus*, for example, than in most of the species considered in this handbook.

Some plant structures, such as fruits, may be much shorter-lived than others, such as stems, and Parry (1962) has suggested that some species of *Apion* may have several broods where they attack these longer-lasting structures. However, more work is needed to establish this.

Economic importance

A numerous group of plant-feeding insects is almost certain to contain some horticultural or agricultural pests, and the weevils are no exception. However, in the families under consideration in this handbook, the pest species tend to be minor nuisances rather than the cause of economic disasters. The Attelabidae include a few relatively unimportant pests of top and soft fruits (Massee 1954; Alford 1984), while the most serious apionid pests are those of leguminous crops, particularly the clover seed weevils (*Apion* (*Protapion*) species), which cause economic losses to red and white clover (*Trifolium pratense* and *T. repens*) grown for seed. *Apion* (*Eutrichapion*) *vorax* is of interest as being one of the few known coleopterous vectors of a virus, in this case two diseases of broad beans (Cockbain *et al*. 1982).

Several species of *Apion* have been 'screened' as suitable for the biological control of various 'weeds' which have been introduced from Europe into North America, Australia, New Zealand and other countries. Over 50 years ago, *A.* (*Exapion*) *ulicis* was assessed for its suitability to control gorse (*Ulex europaeus*). Its potential was considerable as it not only destroys the seeds as a larva but several larvae can inhabit one pod (Davies 1928), and there are plans for a concentrated reintroduction into New Zealand, where *A.* (*Eutrichapion*) *scutellare* is also being studied as an agent for gorse control.

Distribution

Although the broad pattern of the distribution of most weevils is known from published records, details are lacking in many cases. The intensity of recording has been very variable in different areas of the British Isles. Although southern England is generally well recorded, there are some surprising blank spots, for example, Northants and Worcester. Wales is rather poorly recorded except for Glamorgan and Merioneth, and so is Scotland save for the Lothians, some of the Islands and certain 'honeypot' areas of the Highlands. Much work remains to be done in Ireland.

A recording scheme for the weevils considered in this handbook has recently been initiated under the auspices of the Biological Records Centre at ITE's Monks Wood Experimental Station. In this handbook the references to counties, etc., are those of the Watsonian vice counties (Dandy 1969), which preserve a much-needed element of stability compared with the administrative counties, the boundaries of which are so frequently changed.

All distribution records mentioned here are recent and do not include any records of subfossil, Flandrian weevils. Coope (1970) provides an introduction to this subject, which is an active field of current research.

Methods of collecting

Indiscriminate methods of collecting weevils, and other insects, are normally used at three levels in vegetation. The lower branches of trees and shrubs may be jarred with a stick (beaten or tapped) over a beating tray or into a large, stout sweep net. Herbaceous vegetation and tall grassland can be 'swept' using an entomological sweep net. And ground-living weevils can be searched for on hands and knees by the method variously termed 'hand collecting', 'grubbing' or 'grovelling'. More sophisticated methods include the use of insect vacuum nets and heat extraction funnels. Many of the quantitative methods of sampling described by Southwood (1978) can also be used qualitatively.

Weevils are often caught in pitfall traps, though not so frequently as Carabidae and Staphylinidae, and they may be sieved from piles of grass cuttings or other vegetation, or shaken from plant material roded from ditches and ponds. Aquatic Curculionidae may be taken with a normal pond net.

However, all general, or indiscriminate, methods of collecting tend to be less rewarding than working selected plants known to be the hosts of particular species. Some foodplants can be tapped individually into a net or onto a tray. The damage caused by the feeding of adult weevils on foliage is often characteristic and betrays the presence of the insects. Weevils can also be reared, particularly from fruits and galls. Insects so collected are teneral or 'callow' when they emerge and should be kept for a few days to harden and mature. Hymenopterous parasitoids may also be reared, and these should not be discarded as our knowledge of their host ranges is very incomplete. Information on some of the chalcid parasitoids attacking orthocerous weevils is to be found in Fisher (1970).

Although a 'pooter', or insect aspirator, can be used to actually collect weevils from the beating tray or sweep net, it is rarely necessary to do so except in hot weather, when the insects are flying readily. Normally weevils may be placed individually in small specimen tubes, though they are not delicate insects and will not be harmed if mixed together, or with other robust insects, except predaceous species of course. Nevertheless, individual tubing may result in more accurate recording of habitat or host. A fragment of foodplant placed in the tube may be a valuable aid to recording, as well as providing moisture to keep the insects alive. However, too much foliage in a narrow tube may produce condensation enough to kill the weevil placed with it.

Preservation

Unlike many insects, dead weevils do not relax well using standard methods, such as the time-honoured laurel jar. For this reason, many collectors only stun their captures (using ethyl acetate), set them, and then leave them in an atmosphere of ethyl acetate for the final *coup de grace*. Other killing agents may be effective. A very useful alternative to stunning, setting and final killing, particularly where time is limited, as on expedition, is to immerse the killed weevils in a weak (2%) solution of acetic acid. Unlike other methods, this relaxes weevils effectively, though immersion often changes the colour and appearance of scales and setae.

Weevils are usually carded, pinned, or gummed to card 'points'; preservation in 'spirit' (70% ethanol) is an alternative. Pinning is not always easy with small weevils, as the pin may slip on the hard integument or be blunted. Pinned specimens also tend to be more vulnerable than carded one to damage and loss of limbs and antennae. Carding protects appendages and the insects are displayed for identification, measurement and drawing. Aedeagi and spermathecae can be mounted on the card after extraction; these structures are more difficult to preserve in pinned specimens. Pinning does have the advantage that all external characters, including ventral ones, can be readily seen, and this is also true of mounting on card points. Mounting on slips of transparent plastic (instead of card) has been tried as combining the advantages of both carding and pinning, but transparent plastics, particularly when liberally coated with gum, do not normally give a clear enough view of ventral characters to be really useful. It is usually more satisfactory to remove a weevil from its card for detailed examination of the ventral surface.

Gums for mounting weevils may be of various kinds, but domestic adhesives are generally unsuitable and should be avoided. Water-based gums are usually perfectly satisfactory; weevils are easily removed from cards for examination by using a paint-brush and water. However, some collectors prefer spirit-based gum. Most of the 'Coleoptera mounting gums' sold by entomological suppliers are satisfactory, although they often need to be diluted for use.

Set, or carded, weevils are usually kept in storeboxes, or in entomological cabinets. Carding may be 'high' or 'low'. Low-carded weevils are kept on short pins, such as 'Lills' with the cards flat on the surface of the prepared cork (or other material) of the storebox. 'High' carding places the card bearing the insect well up the shaft of the pin. Weevils on low cards are less easily damaged and more of them can be kept in a storebox. High-carded weevils have the data labels more accessible, particularly if more than one label is carried on the pin, and are less vulnerable to attack by pests.

Good data labels are essential if a collection of weevils, or even a single specimen, is to be of any interest to entomologists other than the collector. Even a collector's own collection is useless without good data, in most cases. Most textbooks emphasise locality data, but biological information is often equally important. Data which may be adequate to the collector, for instance a place name without a county, may be of little value to others. Accurate national grid references, particularly six-figure ones, are readily obtainable from any 1:50 000 or 1:25 000 Ordnance Survey map, and are often preferable to topographical data. Many collectors assert that they use parish names as localities, but a study of data labels suggests that in many cases the nearest village or town supplies the name, not the parish in which the collecting locality is situated.

It should always be remembered that the only important data carried by the specimen itself are its identity and sex.

Examination and dissection

It is difficult, if not impossible, to study weevils without at least periodic access to a stereoscopic binocular microscope. Much may be achieved with only low-power magnification, say about × 10 to × 20, but for critical work, high magnifications, to at least × 100 and preferably to × 150 or × 200, are required. Fortunately, most of the characters diagnostic of the specific identity of weevils are external morphological ones. All that is needed for examination is good illumination and the facility to view structures from different angles and with the light incident from different directions. A fine brush, to be used dry or slightly moistened, will be found useful in removing dust or surplus gum which may be obscuring important characters.

Although the proportional size or shape of many structures can be ascertained by observation and comparison, a measuring eyepiece is very useful in making exact observations. Accurate measurements may be made using the engraved scale on a microscope slide in combination with the measuring eyepiece, and less accurate, but still useful, ones by calculation from the power of eyepieces and objectives and the use of the measuring eyepiece.

Dissection of weevils for the study of internal morphology is outside the scope of this handbook. However, dissection to extract the genitalia is often necessary for making accurate specific determinations. The male 'aedeagus', particularly the shape of the penis or median lobe, is important for diagnosis in many cases, and the spermatheca of the female may be helpful in some, though rarely as useful as the male structures. Dissection is best done under the low power of a stereoscopic microscope.

Extraction of the genitalia is invariably easier in freshly-killed weevils than in dried and stored material. In the fresh insect the median lobe can often be pulled out with a pair of fine forceps, though care must be taken not to break or damage it. In most old specimens the abdominal sternites must be carefully cut or broken and the genitalia extracted together with most of the abdomen. This is then soaked for a few minutes in a 10% solution of sodium or potassium hydroxide. The aedeagus or spermatheca can be teased away from the softened abdomen with fine needles or forceps. If left too long in the hydroxide solution, the structures may become pale, soft and attenuated. After dissection of the median lobe or spermatheca, all the remaining sclerotised parts may be washed thoroughly in water and mounted on the card using either the usual gum or, preferably, a transparent mounting medium. Alternatively, the structures may be stored in microvials containing glycerine and attached to the pin bearing the card or specimen, or they can be mounted separately. Only if critical studies are being made will it be necessary to make microscopic mounts. For most work of identification, the

9

dry-mounted structures are perfectly satisfactory. Drawing is generally easier with carded material than with it on microscope slides.

Walsh *et al.* (1975) give much useful advice on methods of collection, preservation and examination, particularly for beginners and collectors with modest resources. A revised and enlarged edition of this work is in preparation.

Adult characteristics

It is difficult to study weevils completely in isolation, without reference to other Coleoptera. Crowson (1956) provides a succinct introduction to the classification and identification of the families of British Coleoptera. The following characters are present in most Curculionoidea. The antennae are more or less clearly clubbed and inserted in cavities or grooves. Geniculate antennae, characteristic of Curculionidae, are seen only in *Nanophyes* of the species considered in the present handbook. The gular sutures (paired in more generalised Coleoptera) are almost always fused in Curculionoidea (Crowson 1956: figs 2, 113). The head is characteristically rostrate in Curculionoidea except in some Anthribidae (and some curculionid subfamilies), but rostra, or some approach to them, are seen in other groups of Coleoptera. In particular, beginners often misidentify *Vincenzellus* and *Rhinosimus* spp. (Salpingidae) as curculionids, because the heads of these beetles are rostrate. The mesothoracic coxal cavities of weevils are nearly always closed externally by sterna, except in *Cimberis*. The abdomen has at least the two basal ventrites connate (rigid and immovable). Many weevils, particularly Curculionidae, bear scales on the body, but scales are absent in the Attelabidae and many species of *Apion*.

A key for the identification of weevils to families is given on pp. 20–21. The reader is referred to Crowson (1956) and Unwin (1984) for general keys to coleopterous families and higher groups. A useful but more popular work for the identification of families is Harde (1984).

Use of the keys

Difficulties abound in both using and writing keys. The taxonomist writes a key with all the species in front of him: the identifier commonly has only a few, perhaps just a single specimen. Some published keys are virtually based on comparative characters — satisfactory enough when all species are available for examination, but almost useless when they are not. The use of some comparative characters is unavoidable, but an attempt has been made in these keys to use them as sparingly as possible. This has meant that differences in the proportions of body characters have been quantified; it follows that a measuring eyepiece for the microscope is desirable, if not essential.

It has rarely been possible to list *all* the characters whereby one taxon differs from another. The keys represent a compromise between reliance on a single character ('beetles black *vs.* beetles blackish-blue') and a detailed and comprehensive diagnosis of all the points of difference. Wherever possible, three or four characters are given for distinguishing species, and more easily seen characters, especially those visible on the upper surface, have been preferred.

The rostrum of weevils is the feeding organ for both sexes, but it is also used in oviposition by many species. The female rostrum is used to construct leaf-rolls in some Attelabidae and to penetrate a wide variety of plant tissues, either deeply or superficially, in all groups. As a consequence, the rostra of the sexes of particular species are often very different. Other secondary sexual differences also abound in weevils. The males of many species have tarsal, tibial or other hooks and claws, which are absent in the female, and are used to hold the sexes together for copulation. It is certain that many of the difficulties encountered by beginners in determining species correctly result from these sexual differences not being widely known, and by confusing the two sexes of one species with two species. Historically, this is certainly true; many of the 'species' described by 18th and 19th century entomologists have turned out to be the other sex of species already known and described. In the present keys, particular attention has been paid to characters by which the sexes may be distinguished, and separate keys to the sexes are provided where this has been thought necessary to make correct determination. This has frequently lengthened the text, but is necessary in many cases for correct determination, which is one of the main aims of these *Handbooks*.

By convention, the length of a weevil is usually given from the apex of the elytra to an imaginary line joining the front margins of the eyes. In many species this is equivalent to the total length excluding the rostrum.

Records of host plants

Much work remains to be done to authenticate records of both hostplants themselves and larval feeding sites. The data given here include some from outside the British Isles, for the sake of completeness. All references to plants are by their scientific names, but vernacular equivalents can be obtained from any standard British flora. The names follow Clapham *et al.* (1987), except for the single species of fungus listed (*Daldinia concentrica*, King Alfred's cakes). A few hostplants which are not British natives, including crop, garden, and introduced species, are listed. A ? before the name of a weevil indicates that there is some doubt that the species feeds on the plant concerned. A ? before the larval feeding site indicates that the weevil is associated with the hostplant but the larval feeding site needs to be confirmed.

Many records are for plants distinguished by their generic names only. These are included for completeness. Records for *Trifolium* spp. and *Trifolium repens*, for instance, may mean that the weevil species concerned feeds only on *T. repens*, or a range of unspecified *Trifolium* species as well as *T. repens*.

Table 1: Plant hosts of British orthocerous weevils and larval feeding sites

Plant host	Weevil species	Feeding site
Alnus glutinosa	*Rhynchites nanus*	Leaf buds
	Deporaus betulae	Leaf rolls
Althea officinalis	*Apion (Aspidapion) soror*	Stems
Althea rosea	*Apion (Aspidapion) radiolus*	Stems
Anthemis spp.	? *Apion (Diplapion) confluens*	Rootstocks
	? *Apion (Omphalapion) sorbi*	Capitula
	? *Apion (Omphalapion) dispar*	? capitula
Arctium spp.	*Apion (Ceratapion) onopordi*	Stems
Astragalus glycyphyllos	*Apion (Pseudotrichapion) astragali*	Flower buds
Betula spp.	*Rhynchites nanus*	Leaf buds
	Rhynchites longiceps	Leaf buds
	Byctiscus betulae	Leaf rolls
	Deporaus mannerheimi	Leaf mines
	Deporaus betulae	Leaf rolls
	Apion (Trichapion) simile	Female catkins
Calamintha spp.	*Apion (Thymapion) flavimanum*	Lower stems
Carduus spp.	*Apion (Ceratapion) onopordi*	Stems
	Apion (Ceratapion) lacertense	? stems
	Apion (Ceratapion) carduorum	Stems
Carpinus betulus	*Tropideres sepicola*	Dead wood

Table 1: (*contd.*)

Plant host	Weevil species	Feeding site
Castanea sativa	*Attelabus nitens*	Leaf rolls
Centaurea spp.	*Apion (Ceratapion) onopordi*	Stems
	Apion (Ceratapion) armatum	? stems
Cirsium spp.	*Apion (Ceratapion) onopordi*	Stems
	Apion (Ceratapion) lacertense	? stems
	Apion (Ceratapion) carduorum	Stems
Cirsium arvense	*Apion (Ceratapion) lacertense*	? stems
	Apion (Ceratapion) carduorum	Stems
Cirsium vulgare	*Apion (Ceratapion) lacertense*	? stems
	Apion (Ceratapion) carduorum	Stems
Clinopodium vulgare	? *Apion (Thymapion) flavimanum*	Lower stems
Cornus sanguinea	? *Rhynchites germanicus*	? shoots
Corylus avellana	*Apoderus coryli*	Leaf rolls
	Byctiscus betulae	Leaf rolls
	Deporaus betulae	Leaf rolls
Crataegus spp.	*Rhynchites bacchus*	Fruits
	Rhynchites caeruleus	Shoots
	Rhynchites pauxillus	Petioles
	Rhynchites aequatus	Fruits
Cytisus scoparius	*Apion (Exapion) fuscirostre*	Pods
	Apion (Pirapion) immune	Stem galls
	Apion (Pirapion) atratulum	Stem galls
Daldinia concentrica	*Platyrhinus resinosus*	Fruiting bodies
Fagus sylvatica	*Tropideres sepicola*	Dead wood
Filago spp.	*Apion (Taphrotopium) brunnipes*	Flower or leaf galls
Filago vulgaris	*Apion (Taphrotopium) brunnipes*	Flower or leaf galls
Fragaria spp.	*Rhynchites germanicus*	Stems, shoots, stolons
Fraxinus excelsior	*Platyrhinus resinosus*	Fungi
Genista spp.	? *Apion (Pirapion) immune*	Stem galls
	Apion (Pirapion) atratulum	Stem galls
Genista anglica	*Apion (Exapion) genistae*	Pods
Genista tinctoria	*Apion (Exapion) difficile*	Pods
Geum spp.	*Rhynchites germanicus*	Stems, shoot, stolons
Gnaphalium spp.	*Apion (Taphrotopium) brunnipes*	Flower or leaf galls
Hedera helix	*Choragus sheppardi*	Dead stems
Hippocrepis comosa	*Apion (Eutrichapion) waltoni*	Stems
Lathyrus spp.	*Apion (Oxystoma) pomonae*	Pods
Lathyrus pratensis	*Apion (Eutrichapion) ervi*	Flower buds
	? *Apion (Eutrichapion) afer*	Vegetative buds
	Apion (Oxystoma) pomonae	Pods
	Apion (Oxystoma) subulatum	Pods
Lavatera spp.	*Apion (Aspidapion) radiolus*	Stems
Leucanthemum vulgare	*Apion (Diplapion) stolidum*	? stems/rootstocks
Limonium bellidifolium	*Apion (Perapion) limonii*	? rootstocks
Limonium binervosum	*Apion (Perapion) limonii*	? rootstocks
Limonium vulgare	*Apion (Perapion) limonii*	? rootstocks
Lotus corniculatus	*Apion (Eutrichapion) loti*	Pods
Lotus uliginosus	*Apion (Synapion) ebeninum*	Stems
	Apion (Eutrichapion) modestum	Pods
Lotus tenuis	? *Apion (Eutrichapion) loti*	Pods
Lythrum portula	*Nanophyes gracilis*	Stem galls
Lythrum salicaria	*Nanophyes marmoratus*	Fruits
Malus spp.	*Rhynchites bacchus*	Fruits
	Rhynchites caeruleus	Shoots
	Rhynchites aequatus	Fruits

Table 1: (*contd.*)

Plant host	Weevil species	Feeding site
Malva spp.	*Apion (Aspidapion) radiolus*	Stems
Malva neglecta	*Apion (Pseudapion) rufirostre*	Fruits
	Apion (Aspidapion) radiolus	Stems
Malva sylvestris	*Apion (Malvapion) malvae*	Fruits
	Apion (Pseudapion) rufirostre	Fruits
	Apion (Aspidapion) aeneum	Stems
	Apion (Aspidapion) radiolus	Stems
Matricaria spp.	*Apion (Diplapion) confluens*	Rootstocks
	? *Apion (Omphalapion) sorbi*	Capitula
	? *Apion (Omphalapion) hookeri*	Capitula
Medicago spp.	? *Apion (Catapion) seniculus*	Stems
	Apion (Pseudotrichapion) pisi	Vegetative buds
	Apion (Eutrichapion) tenue	Stems
	Apion (Protapion) filirostre	Buds
Medicago lupulina	*Apion (Eutrichapion) tenue*	Stems
Melilotus spp.	*Apion (Eutrichapion) meliloti*	Stems
Melilotus alba	*Apion (Eutrichapion) meliloti*	Stems
Melilotus officinalis	*Apion (Eutrichapion) meliloti*	Stems
Mentha spp.	*Apion (Thymapion) vicinum*	Stem galls
Mentha aquatica	*Apion (Thymapion) vicinum*	Stem galls
Mercurialis annua	*Apion (Kalcapion) semivittatum*	Stems
Mercurialis perennis	*Apion (Kalcapion) pallipes*	Stems
Mespilus germanica	*Rhynchites pauxillus*	Petioles
	Rhynchites aequatus	Fruits
Onobrychis viciifolia	*Apion (Eutrichapion) intermedium*	Stems
	Apion (Eutrichapion) reflexum	? flower galls
Ononis repens	*Apion (Eutrichapion) ononis*	Pods
	Apion (Protapion) ononicola	Pods
Ononis spinosa	*Apion (Eutrichapion) ononis*	Pods
	Apion (Protapion) ononicola	Pods
Origanum vulgare	*Apion (Thymapion) flavimanum*	Lower stems
Pinus sylvestris	*Cimberis attelaboides*	Male flowers
Polygonum aviculare agg.	*Apion (Perapion) lemoroi*	Stems
Populus spp.	*Rhynchites tomentosus*	Leaf buds
Populus alba	*Byctiscus populi*	Leaf rolls
Populus tremula	*Rhynchites tomentosus*	Leaf buds
	Byctiscus populi	Leaf rolls
Potentilla spp.	*Rhynchites germanicus*	Stems, shoots, stolons
Prunella vulgaris	*Apion (Thymapion) cineraceum*	? roots
Prunus spp.	*Rhynchites auratus*	Fruits
	Rhynchites bacchus	Fruits
	Rhynchites caeruleus	Shoots
	Rhynchites aequatus	Fruits
Prunus spinosa	*Rhynchites auratus*	Fruits
	Rhynchites caeruleus	Shoots
	Rhynchites pauxillus	Petioles
	Rhynchites aequatus	Fruits
Pyrus spp.	*Rhynchites caeruleus*	Shoots
	Rhynchites longiceps	Leaf buds
Quercus spp.	*Tropideres sepicola*	Dead wood
	Attelabus nitens	Leaf rolls
	Rhynchites cavifrons	Twigs
	Rhynchites olivaceus	Twigs
	Rhynchites sericeus	Leaf rolls (brood parasite)

Table 1: (*contd.*)

Plant host	Weevil species	Feeding site
	? Rhynchites germanicus	? shoots
	Rhynchites interpunctatus	(unknown)
	Rhynchites aeneovirens	Buds
Reseda lutea	*Bruchela rufipes*	Fruits
Rosa spp.	*Rhynchites germanicus*	Shoots, stems, stolons
Rubus spp.	*Rhynchites germanicus*	Shoots, stems, stolons
Rumex (Rumex) spp.	*Apion (Perapion) hydrolapathi*	Stems
	Apion (Perapion) violaceum	Stems
	Apion (Perapion) curtirostre	Stems
	Apion (s.str.) frumentarium	Rootstocks, etc.
Rumex acetosa	*Apion (Perapion) violaceum*	Stems
	Apion (Perapion) affine	? inflorescence galls
	Apion (Perapion) curtirostre	Stems
	Apion (s.str.) cruentatum	Lower stems, etc.
Rumex acetosella agg.	*Apion (Perapion) affine*	? inflorescence galls
	Apion (Perapion) marchicum	Root galls
	Apion (Perapion) curtirostre	Stems
	? Apion (s.str.) cruentatum	Lower stems, etc.
	Apion (s.str.) rubens	Petiole galls
	Apion (s.str.) rubiginosum	Root galls
	Apion (s.str.) haematodes	Rootstocks
Rumex conglomeratus	*Apion (s.str.) frumentarium*	Rootstocks, etc.
Rumex crispus	*Apion (Perapion) hydrolapathi*	Stems
	Apion (s.str.) frumentarium	Rootstocks, etc.
Rumex hydrolapathum	*Apion (Perapion) hydrolapathi*	Stems
	Apion (s.str.) frumentarium	Rootstocks, etc.
Rumex obtusifolius	*Apion (Perapion) hydrolapathi*	Stems
Salix spp.	*Rhynchites tomentosus*	Leaf buds
	Rhynchites nanus	Leaf buds
	Rhynchites longiceps	Leaf buds
	? Rhynchites germanicus	? stems
	Apion (Melanapion) minimum	Inquiline in *Pontania* galls
Salix caprea	*Rhynchites tomentosus*	Leaf buds
Salix repens	*Rhynchites tomentosus*	Leaf buds
Salix viminalis	*Rhynchites tomentosus*	Leaf buds
Sanguisorba officinalis	*Rhynchites germanicus*	Stems, shoots, stolons
Sedum spp.	*? Apion (Perapion) sedi*	Leaf/stem galls
Sedum acre	*Apion (Perapion) sedi*	Leaf/stem mines
Sedum anglicum	*Apion (Perapion) sedi*	Leaf/stem galls
Sempervivum tectorum	*? Apion (Perapion) sedi*	Leaf/stem galls
Sorbus aucuparia	*Rhynchites cupreus*	Fruits
	Rhynchites aequatus	Fruits
Sorbus torminalis	*Rhynchites caeruleus*	Shoots
Thymus spp.	*Apion (Thymapion) atomarium*	Stem galls
Trifolium spp.	*Apion (Catapion) seniculus*	Stems
	Apion (Catapion) curtisii	Root galls
	Apion (Eutrichapion) virens	Stems
	? Apion (Protapion) difforme	(unknown)
	? Apion (Protapion) schoenherri	(unknown)
	Apion (Protapion) assimile	Flower heads
	? Apion (Protapion) ryei	(unknown)
Trifolium arvense	*Apion (Protapion) dissimile*	Inflorescences
Trifolium aureum	*Apion (Catapion) pubescens*	Stem galls
	? Apion (Protapion) nigritarse	Flower heads
Trifolium campestre	*Apion (Catapion) pubescens*	Stem galls

Table 1: (*contd.*)

Plant host	Weevil species	Feeding site
	? Apion (Protapion) nigritarse	Flower heads
Trifolium dubium	*Apion (Catapion) pubescens*	Stem galls
	? Apion (Protapion) nigritarse	Flower heads
Trifolium fragiferum	*? Apion (Catapion) curtisii*	Root galls
Trifolium hybridum	*Apion (Catapion) seniculus*	Stems
	Apion (Protapion) dichroum	Flower heads
	Apion (Protapion) assimile	Flower heads
Trifolium medium	*Apion (Protapion) trifolii*	Flower heads
	Apion (Protapion) assimile	Flower heads
Trifolium ochroleucon	*Apion (Protapion) assimile*	Flower heads
Trifolium pratense	*Apion (Protapion) varipes*	? flowers, ? galls
	Apion (Protapion) trifolii	Flower heads
	Apion (Protapion) apricans	Flower heads
	Apion (Protapion) assimile	Flower heads
Trifolium repens	*? Apion (Catapion) curtisii*	Root galls
	Apion (Eutrichapion) virens	Stems
	Apion (Protapion) dichroum	Flower heads
	? Apion (Protapion) laevicolle	? galls
Tripleurospermum spp.	*Apion (Diplapion) confluens*	Rootstocks
	Apion (Omphalapion) hookeri	Capitula
Ulex spp.	*Apion (Exapion) ulicis*	Pods
Ulex europaeus	*Apion (Exapion) ulicis*	Pods
	Apion (Pirapion) atratulum	? stem galls
	Apion (Eutrichapion) scutellare	Stem galls
Ulex gallii	*? Apion (Eutrichapion) scutellare*	Stem galls
Ulex minor	*Apion (Eutrichapion) scutellare*	Stem galls
Urtica dioica	*Apion (Taeniapion) urticarium*	Stems
Urtica urens	*? Apion (Taeniapion) urticarium*	Stems
Vicia spp.	*Apion (Pseudotrichapion) punctigerum*	Pods
	Apion (Pseudotrichapion) aethiops	Stem galls
	Apion (Eutrichapion) viciae	Flowers
	Apion (Eutrichapion) spencii	(unknown)
	Apion (Eutrichapion) ervi	Flower buds
	Apion (Eutrichapion) vorax	Flowers
	Apion (Eutrichapion) gyllenhali	Stem galls
	Apion (Oxystoma) pomonae	Pods
	Apion (Oxystoma) craccae	Pods
	Apion (Oxystoma) cerdo	Pods
Vicia cracca	*Apion (Pseudotrichapion) aethiops*	Stem galls
	Apion (Eutrichapion) viciae	Flowers
	Apion (Eutrichapion) spencii	(unknown)
	Apion (Eutrichapion) gyllenhali	Stem galls
	Apion (Oxystoma) pomonae	Pods
	Apion (Oxystoma) cerdo	Pods
Vicia faba	*Apion (Eutrichapion) vorax*	Flowers
Vicia sepium	*Apion (Pseudotrichapion) punctigerum*	Pods
	Apion (Pseudotrichapion) aethiops	Stem galls
	Apion (Oxystoma) pomonae	Pods

Check list

A few changes to the list of Kloet & Hincks (1977) are necessary because of additional species, changes in nomenclature and clarification of relationships, but the list remains substantially as the earlier one.

The following prefix and suffixes are used.

Textual prefix:

S   subgenus

Suffixes:

†   extinct
?†   probably extinct
+   occurring only under artificial conditions
H   homonym
M   misidentification

For a discussion of the nomenclatural points raised by these suffixes, the reader is referred to Kloet & Hincks (1977).

CURCULIONOIDEA

NEMONYCHIDAE
RHINOMACERIDAE

CIMBERIS des Gozis, 1881
  RHINOMACER sensu auctt., not Fabricius, 1877
attelaboides Fabricius, 1787

ANTHRIBIDAE
  PLATYRHINIDAE
  PLATYSTOMATIDAE
  PLATYSTOMIDAE

ANTHRIBINAE

PLATYRHINUS Clairville, 1798
  ANTHRIBUS auctt., not Müller, O.F., 1764
  PLATYRRHINUS Fowler, 1891 (misspelling)
resinosus (Scopoli, 1763)
  latirostris (Fabricius, 1775)

TROPIDERES Schoenherr, 1823

S. TROPIDERES s.str.
sepicola (Fabricius, 1792)

S. DISSOLEUCAS Jordan, K., 1925
niveirostris (Fabricius, 1798)

PLATYSTOMOS Schneider, 1791
  ANTHRIBUS Müller, O.F., 1764
  MACROCEPHALUS Olivier, 1789, not Swederus, 1787
  PLATYSTOMUS auctt. (misspelling)
albinus (Linnaeus, 1758)

ANTHRIBUS Müller, O.F., 1764
  BRACHYTARSUS Schoenherr, 1823
fasciatus (Forster, 1771)
nebulosus (Forster, 1771)
  variegatus (Fourcroy, 1785)
  varius (Fabricius, 1787)

CHORAGINAE

ARAECERUS Schoenherr, 1823
  AREOCERUS auctt. (misspelling)
fasciculatus (Degeer, 1775)   +

CHORAGUS Kirby, W., 1819
sheppardi Kirby, W., 1819

URODONTIDAE

BRUCHELA Dejean, 1821
  URODON Schoenherr, 1823
rufipes (Olivier, 1790)

ATTELABIDAE

ATTELABINAE

ATTELABUS Linnaeus, 1758
nitens (Scopoli, 1763)
  curculionoides Linnaeus, 1763

APODERINAE

APODERUS Olivier, 1807
coryli (Linnaeus, 1758)

RHYNCHITINAE

RHYNCHITES Schneider, 1791

S. RHYNCHITES s.str.
auratus (Scopoli, 1763)   †
bacchus (Linnaeus, 1758)   †
caeruleus (Degeer, 1775)
cupreus (Linnaeus, 1758)

S. LASIORHYNCHITES Jekel, 1860
cavifrons Gyllenhal, 1833
  pubescens sensu auctt., not (Fabricius, 1775)
olivaceus Gyllenhal, 1833
  ophthalmicus sensu auctt. Brit., not Stephens, 1831
  sericeus sensu Fowler, 1890, not Herbst, 1797
sericeus Herbst, 1797   ?†
  olivaceus sensu Hincks, 1951, not Gyllenhal, 1833
  ophthalmicus Stephens, 1831

S. NEOCOENORRHINUS Voss, 1951
  CAENORHINUS auctt., not Thomson, C.G. 1859*
  COENORHINUS Voss, 1932
aeneovirens (Marsham, 1802)
aequatus (Linnaeus, 1767)
germanicus Herbst, 1797
  minutus sensu Thomson, C.G., 1866, not Herbst, 1797
interpunctatus Stephens, 1831
pauxillus Germar, 1824

S. PSELAPHORHYNCHITES Schilsky, 1903
longiceps Thomson, C.G., 1888
  harwoodi Joy, 1911
nanus (Paykull, 1792)
tomentosus Gyllenhal, 1839
  uncinatus Thomson, C.G., 1865

BYCTISCUS Thomson, C.G., 1859
betulae (Linnaeus, 1758)
  betuleti (Fabricius, 1792)
populi (Linnaeus, 1758)

DEPORAUS Samouelle, 1819
betulae (Linnaeus, 1758)

*Caenorhinus Thomson is a synonym of *Deporaus* Samouelle s. *Hydrodeporaus* Voss

17

mannerheimi (Hummel, 1823)
  megacephalus (Germar, 1824)

APIONIDAE

APIONINAE

APION Herbst, 1797

S. PERAPION Wagner, H., 1907
affine Kirby, W., 1808
curtirostre Germar, 1817
  brevirostre sensu Kirby, W., 1808, not Herbst, 1797
  humile Germar, 1817
hydrolapathi (Marsham, 1802)
lemoroi Brisout, 1880
limonii Kirby, W., 1808
marchicum Herbst, 1797
sedi Germar, 1818
violaceum Kirby, W., 1808

S. MALVAPION Hoffmann, 1958
malvae (Fabricius, 1775)

S. PSEUDAPION Schilsky, 1906
rufirostre (Fabricius, 1775)

S. ASPIDAPION Schilsky, 1901
aeneum (Fabricius, 1775)
radiolus (Marsham, 1802)
soror Rey, 1895
  foveatoscutellatum Wagner, H., 1906

S. KALCAPION Schilsky, 1906
pallipes Kirby, W., 1808
semivittatum Gyllenhal, 1833

S. TAENIAPION Schilsky, 1906
urticarium (Herbst, 1784)

S. EXAPION Bedel, 1885
difficile Herbst, 1797
  kiesenwetteri Desbrochers, 1870
fuscirostre (Fabricius, 1775)
genistae Kirby, W., 1811
ulicis (Forster, 1771)

S. APION s.s.
  ERYTHRAPION Schilsky, 1906
cruentatum Walton, J., 1844
  sanguineum Stephens, 1839   M
  desideratum Sharp, 1918
frumentarium (Linnaeus, 1758)
  sanguineum (Degeer, 1775)
  miniatum Germar, 1833
haematodes Kirby, W., 1808
  frumentarium (Paykull, 1792)   M
  brachypterum Sharp, 1918
  fraudator Sharp, 1918
rubens Stephens, 1839
rubiginosum Grill, 1893
  sanguineum auctt., not Degeer, 1775   M

S. THYMAPION Deville, 1924
atomarium Kirby, W., 1808
  minutissimum sensu auctt. Brit., not Rosenhauer, 1856

18

serpyllicola sensu auctt. Brit., not Wencker, 1864
cineraceum Wencker, 1864
   annulipes sensu auctt., not Wencker, 1864
   millum sensu Bach, 1854, not Gyllenhal, 1833
flavimanum Gyllenhal, 1833
vicinum Kirby, W., 1808

S. CATAPION Schilsky, 1906
curtisii Stephens, 1831
   curtulum Desbrochers, 1870
pubescens Kirby, W., 1811
seniculus Kirby, W., 1808

S. DIPLAPION Reitter, 1916
confluens Kirby, W., 1808
stolidum Germar, 1817

S. TAPHROTOPIUM Reitter, 1916
brunnipes Boheman, 1839
   laevigatum Kirby, W., 1808, not (Paykull, 1792)

S. CERATAPION Schilsky, 1901
armatum Gerstaecker, 1854
carduorum Kirby, W., 1808
lacertense Tottenham, 1941
   dentirostre sensu auctt. Brit., not Gerstaecker, 1854
onopordi Kirby, W., 1808

S. OMPHALAPION Schilsky, 1901
dispar Germar, 1817
hookeri Kirby, W., 1808
sorbi (Fabricius, 1792)
   laevigatum (Paykull, 1792)   H

S. SYNAPION Schilsky, 1902
ebeninum Kirby, W., 1808

S. PIRAPION Reitter, 1916
atratulum Germar, 1817
   striatum (Marsham, 1802)   H
immune Kirby, W., 1808

S. MELANAPION Wagner, H., 1930
minimum Herbst, 1797

S. TRICHAPION Wagner, H., 1912
simile Kirby, W., 1811

S. PSEUDOTRICHAPION Wagner, H., 1932
   S. APION s.str. sensu auctt.   M
aethiops Herbst, 1797
astragali (Paykull, 1800)   H
pisi (Fabricius, 1801)
punctigerum (Paykull, 1792)

S. EUTRICHAPION Reitter, 1916
afer Gyllenhal, 1833
   platalea sensu auctt., not Germar, 1817
   unicolor sensu auctt., not Kirby, W., 1808
ervi Kirby, W., 1808
gyllenhali Kirby, W., 1808
   unicolor Kirby, W., 1808
intermedium Eppelsheim, 1875
loti Kirby, W., 1808
meliloti Kirby, W., 1808

modestum Germar, 1817
  sicardi sensu auctt. Brit., not Desbrochers, 1893
ononis Kirby, W., 1808
reflexum Gyllenhal, 1833
  livescerum Gyllenhal, 1833
scutellare Kirby, W., 1811
spencii Kirby, W., 1808
tenue Kirby, W., 1808
viciae (Paykull, 1800)
virens Herbst, 1797
vorax Herbst, 1797
waltoni Stephens, 1839

S. OXYSTOMA Duméril, 1806
cerdo Gerstaecker, 1854
craccae (Linnaeus, 1767)
pomonae (Fabricius, 1798)
  opeticum sensu auctt. Brit., not Bach, 1854
subulatum Kirby, W., 1808

S. PROTAPION Schilsky, 1908
apricans Herbst, 1797
assimile Kirby, W., 1808
  bohemani sensu Bedel, 1885, not Thomson, C.G., 1865
dichroum Bedel, 1886
  flavipes sensu (Paykull, 1792), not (Fabricius, 1775)
difforme Germar, 1818
dissimile Germar, 1817
filirostre Kirby, W., 1808
  cantianum Wagner, H., 1906
laevicolle Kirby, W., 1811
nigritarse Kirby, W., 1808
ononicola Bach, 1854
  bohemani Thomson, C.G., 1865
ryei Blackburn, 1874
schoenherri Boheman, 1839
trifolii (Linnaeus, 1768)
  aestivum Germar, 1817
varipes Germar, 1817

NANOPHYINAE

NANOPHYES Schoenherr, 1838
gracilis Redtenbacher, 1849
marmoratus (Goeze, 1777)
  lythri (Fabricius, 1787)

Key to the families of British weevils (Curculionoidea)

1   Rostrum very short *and* antennae straight (orthocerous, not geniculate) with a loose, 3-segmented club; pronotum with a basal or sub-basal keel which extends forwards on each side forming an incomplete side border 2

—   If rostrum very short then antennae geniculate with a compact (3-segmented) club; if pronotum with a basal or sub-basal keel, this does not extend forwards to form a side border 3

2   Second tarsal segment embracing third (fig. 11); elytral striae well marked; pronotal transverse carina usually sub-basal (figs. 13, 16); scutellum usually distinct; base of pronotum straight (figs. 12, 21) or with lateral angles wanting (figs. 13, 16), but without a median expansion; [8 spp., associated with dead wood, fungi, Coccidae or stored products] . . . . **ANTHRIBIDAE**

—   Second tarsal segment not embracing third (fig. 26); elytral striae (except one) wanting; pronotal transverse carina basal; scutellum concealed; base of pronotum sinuate, with an expanded median portion about half as wide as extreme breadth (fig. 27); [1 sp., associated with *Reseda lutea*]. . . . . **URODONTIDAE**
3   All abdominal sternites free; elytra without striae; labrum free; antennae straight with a weak, loose, 3-segmented club; [1 sp., associated with *Pinus sylvestris*] . . . .
. . . . **NEMONYCHIDAE**
—   At least two basal sternites connate; elytra usually striate; labrum not fully free; antennae geniculate, or if straight then club more obvious, usually compact, 3-segmented 4
4   Antennae straight (orthocerous) (e.g. fig. 28); body usually without scales, glabrous, strongly to weakly shining 6
—   Antennae geniculate (e.g. fig. 78); body often with scales, not shining. 5
5   Trochanters long; pronotum at base almost as wide as elytra, strongly narrowed to head, sides almost straight, rostrum long; [Nanophyinae: 2 spp., associated with Lythraceae] .
. . . . **APIONIDAE** (in part)
—   Trochanters short; if pronotum at base almost as wide as elytra then pronotum not strongly narrowed to head, or sides curved or rostrum short. 7
6   Antennal club loose, segments distinct; tarsal claws connate or mandibles toothed on outer side; elytra usually somewhat depressed, not so curved at sides and not pear-shaped; trochanters short, if long then rostrum very short; [18 spp., mostly associated with broad-leaved trees]. . . . . **ATTELABIDAE**
—   Antennal club compact, segments not obvious; tarsal claws free; mandibles not toothed on outer side; elytra seldom depressed, usually more rounded at sides and often pear-shaped; trochanters long; [Apioninae; 84 spp., mostly associated with herbs] . . . .
. . . . **APIONIDAE** (in greater part)
7   Rostrum nearly always distinct, often long; tibiae without dentate outer edges; pronotum without distinct side borders; [*c.* 425 spp., associated with a wide range of plants and plant products] . . . . **CURCULIONIDAE***
—   Rostrum absent, not distinct, or very short; tibiae with dentate outer edges or pronotum with distinct side borders. 8
8   Tarsi with 4th segment very small; segment 1 shorter than 2, 3 and 4 together; head clearly narrower than pronotum; often less elongate, short-oval species; [*c.* 60 spp., associated with the bark or dead wood of trees, broadleaved and especially conifers] . . . .
. . . . **SCOLYTIDAE‡**
—   Tarsi with 4th segment at least half as long as 3rd, segment 1 longer than 2, 3 and 4 together; head as broad as, or scarcely narrower than, pronotum; elongate and very cylindrical species; [1 native sp., but other imported spp. sometimes found, in felled broadleaved trees and stumps]. . . . . **PLATYPODIDAE†**

*Not yet keyed in this series of handbooks
†Keyed by Duffy (1953)
‡Keyed by Duffy (1953), but with additional species added to the British fauna since then.

Family Nemonychidae

This small family of five genera is now generally regarded as distinct (Crowson, 1950–1954 (1967), 1956; Kloet & Hincks, 1977), although it is still occasionally treated as a subfamily of Curculionidae (*s.lat.*) closely related to Rhynchitinae, Attelabinae and Apoderinae (e.g. Dieckmann, 1974; Lohse, 1981). Three species in three different genera occur in Europe, but neither *Nemonyx lepturoides* (F.) nor *Doydirhynchus austriacus* (Olivier) occurs in the British Isles. It has recently been shown that *Nemonyx* differs in many respects from other genera in the family and that possibly two families should be recognised. If this is so, *Cimberis* should be placed in Cimberidae (Crowson, 1985).

Genus **Cimberis** Des Gozis

The single European species in this genus occurs in the British Isles (fig. 1).

— Elongate, derm black, dark brown, or slightly brassy, slightly shining. Upper surface covered in long, semi-recumbent pubescence varying in colour from nearly white to dark yellowish-brown. Legs and antennae red to yellowish, tarsi darker. Rostrum short (shorter than the pronotum), dilated at apex and also at base (fig. 5). Antennae long, about as long as the pronotum, head and rostrum together, orthocerous, with the club very ill-defined (last four segments broader apically than remainder). Head transverse, nearly as broad as pronotum, eyes prominent. Pronotum slightly longer than broad, gently rounded at sides. Elytra parallel-sided, about $2\frac{1}{2} \times$ longer than broad, distinctly, closely and confusedly punctured, striae absent. Length 3·0–5·5 mm. . . . . . **attelaboides** Fabricius
   Male with fore tibiae (and to a lesser extent the mid tibiae) strongly bent inwards apically, with an apical or subapical tooth (fig. 6); eighth segment of antennae broader at apex (fig. 8); ventral surface of abdomen without median line of yellowish setae. Female with all tibiae straight, or nearly so, without apical or subapical teeth (fig. 7); eighth segment of antennae narrower at apex (fig. 9); ventral surface of abdomen with a median line of dense, yellowish setae.
   In coniferous forests, and plantations containing Scots Pine. On Pinus sylvestris, *with other hosts in Britain requiring confirmation. Larvae in the male flowers, feeding on pollen, but biological details scanty. Formerly probably only in relict Caledonian pine forest, but now widely distributed because of the planting of the host, though still not of general occurrence. From Dorset eastwards and northwards to Elgin and Easterness but not known from further north in Scotland, nor from Wales or Ireland. All Europe, including northern Scandinavia, Asia Minor.*

Family Anthribidae

This well-characterised family is poorly represented in the British Isles and much richer in species in the tropics. However, our few species demonstrate the wide range of larval feeding habits within the family. Anthribids which bore into dead wood, which feed on fungi, which are predators of Coccidae, and which are seed-feeders, are represented in our fauna, the last by an introduced and synanthropic species. The family contains two subfamilies. All our species are uncommon and most are decidedly rare.

Key to subfamilies

1   Antennae inserted at the side of the head, basal segment covered proximally by lateral expansion of the head and so not visible from above (fig. 10); transverse carina of pronotum, if present, more remote from the posterior margin, separated from it by a distance much greater than the width of the fore tibia (figs 13, 16); larger species, length 3·3–13·0 mm; if shorter than 3·5 mm then first segment of tarsi shorter, not more than 3 × longer than broad; [species not saltatorial] . . . . **Anthribinae**
—   Antennae inserted on the dorsal surface of the head, the whole basal segment and its articulation clearly visible from above (fig. 22); transverse carina of pronotum, if present, close to posterior margin of pronotum, separated from it by a distance about equal to the width of fore tibia (fig. 21); size smaller, length 1·4–4·5 mm; if longer than 3·5 mm then first segment of tarsi very long, more than 3 × longer than broad; [saltatorial species] . . . . **Choraginae**

Subfamily Anthribinae

Key to genera

1   Pronotum with a sub-basal transverse carina (figs 13, 16) (if somewhat obsolete in middle then size large, length 8–13 mm). 2

— Pronotum without a trace of a sub-basal transverse carina 3
2 Size smaller, length not more than 5·5 mm; pronotum not produced laterally to form a bluntly and shallowly bilobed projection or tooth, not irregularly and coarsely ridged and pitted, sub-basal carina entire (figs 13, 16); eyes not bounded on their inner edge by a distinct raised ridge .... **Tropideres** Schoenherr
— Size larger, length not less than 7 mm (normally 8–13 mm); pronotum produced laterally into a blunt and very shallowly bilobed projection or tooth (fig. 12), coarsely pitted and with irregular ridges, particularly at sides, sub-basal carina incomplete, interrupted for a short distance in the middle; eyes very prominent and bounded on their inner edge by a distinct crest or raised ridge .... **Platyrhinus** Clairville
3 Antennae short, shorter than the pronotum; head short, rostrum not dilated at or in front of antennal insertion; size smaller, length 2·5–5 mm .... **Anthribus** Müller
— Antennae long, longer than the pronotum; head (with rostrum) long, strongly dilated at, or just in front of, antennal insertion; size larger, length 7–10 mm . . .**Platystomos** Schneider

Genus **Platyrhinus** Clairville

The only European species of this genus, to which the name *Anthribus* has been applied (Kloet & Hincks, 1977), occurs in Britain.

— For description, see key to genera .... **resinosus** (Scopoli) (fig. 2)
Male abdomen, with venter shallowly and longitudinally excavated; antennae longer, longer than the breadth of head across eyes, segments 3 and 4 more elongate, about 3× longer than broad. Female abdomen without a shallow and longitudinal ventral excavation; antennae shorter, only as long as, or shorter than, the breadth of head across eyes; segments 3 and 4 less elongate, little more than twice as long as broad.
In woods, particularly on dead ash (Fraxinus) but recorded from dead wood of other trees. Larvae in the fungus Daldinia concentrica, which usually grows on Ash. Not common, but widely distributed and one of the least rare of our anthribids in England. S. Devon, N. and S. Somerset and E. Kent northwards to Mid-W. Yorks.; Glamorgan; 'Tay district' of Scotland (Sharp). Not recorded from Ireland. Europe to eastern Siberia; North Africa.

Genus **Tropideres** Schoenherr

Only two species of this genus occur in the British Isles, although eleven are known from France. *T. albirostris* (Herbst), recorded by Stephens (1831), but unknown in Britain for the last 150 years, has been omitted from both Kloet & Hincks (1977) and this handbook.

Key to species

1 Pronotum on disc with two distinct, pointed, conical bunches of raised setae (arranged side by side); pronotum gradually rounded basad from transverse carina (fig. 16); head narrower, rostrum longer; elytra with large, irregular, black, transversely-oval patch just behind middle; [length 3·0–4·7 mm]......................... **sepicola** (Fabricius)
Male with the mid femora with a fine tooth beneath; antennae longer. Female with the mid femora unarmed; antennae shorter.
In old primary woodlands on dead branches of Quercus, Carpinus, Fagus, etc.; larvae in dead wood. Very local and rare, but comparatively less rare than T. niveirostris during the 20th century. N. and S. Hants, E. Kent, N. Essex, Hunts, Hereford and Leicester. Not recorded from Wales, Scotland or Ireland.
— Disc of pronotum with an obscure, transverse, shallow depression in front of a narrow, slightly raised area, but without distinct bunches of raised setae; pronotum abruptly contracted basad from transverse carina (fig. 13); head broader, rostrum shorter; elytra somewhat tessellated with dark and pale areas but without large, black, oval patch just behind middle; [length 3·3–5·4 mm]......................... **niveirostris** (Fabricius)

Male with the mid and hind tibiae armed at apex with a curved tooth (fig. 14), directed inwards; antennae longer, segments 7 and 8 at least twice as long as broad. Female with the mid and hind tibiae unarmed at apex (fig. 15); antennae shorter, segments 7 and 8 about 1.5 × longer than broad.

In woods and old, neglected hedges, on dead branches of a variety of trees and shrubs; larvae in the dead wood. Rare, very scarce this century, though apparently a little less so in the nineteenth. Dorset, S. Hants, E. and W. Kent, W. Gloucester and Leicester. Not recorded from Wales, Scotland or Ireland.

Genus **Platystomos** Schneider

Our single species is the only one known in this genus from northern Europe.

— A large and conspicuous species, characterised by the white pubescence of the head and apex of the elytra (fig. 3). Other descriptive features as in the generic key .. **albinus** (Linnaeus)
    Male with the antennae much longer, reaching at least to the middle of the elytra and scarcely shorter than the whole body. Female with the antennae shorter, reaching only a short way beyond the base of the pronotum.
    Usually in woods, on dead and dying trees; the larvae in the dead wood. Very local and usually rare. Dorset to E. Kent and northwards to S. Lincoln and Durham (formerly), but recorded from only 11 vice counties. Not recorded from Wales, Scotland or Ireland.

Genus **Anthribus** Müller

Two of about ten species of this genus, more familiar under the name of *Brachytarsus* Schoenherr, recorded from Europe occur in the British Isles. Ecologically, they are chiefly notable for being predators of Coccinae (= Lecaniinae) as larvae.

Key to species

1 Pronotum with reflexed lateral margins throughout, more strongly transverse (0·64–0·68 × as long as broad); elytral striae coarse; elytra red with black markings, tessellated, less rounded, sub-truncate at apex (fig. 17); (length 3·3–4·5 mm) . . . . **fasciatus** (Forster)
    Male with antennae very slightly longer, the eighth segment quadrate or slightly transverse; tarsal claws of the fore and mid legs with the inner one of each pair little more than half the length of the outer (fig. 18). Female with the antennae a trifle shorter, the eighth segment distinctly transverse; tarsal claws of the fore and mid legs with the inner one of each pair fully, or nearly, as long as the outer (fig. 19).
    In hedges, woods, etc. on a wide variety of trees. Larval hosts (Coccinae) not well recorded in Britain. Widely distributed but seldom common in England from Dorset eastwards to E. Kent and northwards to Chester and S. Lancaster. Wales: Glamorgan and Denbigh. Scotland: Berwick. Not recorded from Ireland. Europe, N. Africa.

— Pronotum with reflexed lateral margin evident only weakly at base, less strongly transverse (0·72–0·79 × as long as broad); elytral striae finer; elytra black with small batches of paler pubescence, more gradually rounded at apex (fig. 20); [length 2·5–4·6 mm] . . . .
. . . . **nebulosus** (Forster)
    Male with antennae a little longer, segments 5–8 distinctly elongate. Female with the antennae slightly shorter, segments 5–8 quadrate, or only very slightly elongate.
    In woods, hedges and plantations on a variety of broadleaved and coniferous trees and shrubs. The larvae are predators of Coccinae, but the hosts are not well known in Britain. Local and uncommon, but widely distributed in England from N. and S. Somerset eastwards to E. Kent and northwards to Cumberland and Westmorland. Wales: Denbigh. In Scotland from the Borders to Mid Perth. Not known from Ireland. Europe to Siberia.

Subfamily Choraginae

Key to genera

1   Pronotum with a complete transverse carina close to base (fig. 21); fore and mid tarsi short, much shorter than the tibiae, the first segment not more than 2·5 × longer than broad; elytra sparsely and uniformly pubescent, the pubescence not forming a pattern; pygidium not visible from above, third antennal segment shorter than the second; size smaller, 1·4–2·5 mm . . . . **Choragus** Kirby

—   Pronotum without a transverse carina close to base (but with posterior margin somewhat raised, shining); fore and mid tarsi long, with claws as long as, or very little shorter than, the tibiae, the first segment about 3 × longer than broad; elytra more densely pubescent, the pubescence not uniform and producing a light and dark pattern, tessellated towards apex; pygidium clearly visible from above; third antennal segment longer than second; size larger, 3·8–4·5 mm . . . . **Araecerus** Schoenherr

Genus **Choragus** Kirby

Only one of the two species in this genus which are recorded from northern Europe occurs in the British Isles.

—   A very small species occurring outdoors. For characteristics, see generic key **sheppardi** Kirby
     No secondary sexual characters are known by which to distinguish males from females (Cymorek 1963).
     In hedges and woods on old, dead Ivy (Hedera helix); *the larvae in the rotten, fungus-infested wood. Local and usually rare, but widely distributed throughout England from W. Cornwall to E. Kent and northwards to N.E. York. Also recorded from Wales (Glamorgan), Scotland (Lanark) and Ireland (Dublin). Central and southern Europe.*

Genus **Araecerus Schoenherr**

A genus of the Oriental region, from which one species has become well established in Europe and elsewhere.

—   A synanthropic species. For characteristics, see generic key . . . . **fasciculatus** (Degeer)
     Male with the pygidium rounded, blunt posteriorly and rounded or subtruncate in lateral view (fig. 23). Female with the pygidium triangular, pointed posteriorly and produced in lateral view (fig. 24).
     Introduced; probably a native of the Oriental region. Synanthropic, in food factories (formerly) and warehouses. etc, associated with foodstuffs; a stored products pest. Larvae in coffee and cocoa beans, nuts, etc. Of wide occurrence but seldom seen because of effective hygiene and control measures. England to Scotland (Edinburgh); not recorded from Wales or Ireland. Almost cosmopolitan.

Family Urodontidae

Family status for this group has recently been supported by Crowson (1984), in agreement with the proposal first made by Hoffmann (1945). Other authors have placed the group variously in the Bruchidae, Anthribidae or Nemonychidae. Brandl (1981) places *Urodon* (= *Bruchela*) in a subfamily Urodoninae (*sic*) of Bruchidae. On both adult and larval characters, *Bruchela* is curculionoid, not chrysomeloid (Crowson, 1984).

Genus **Bruchela** Dejean

The genus is the only representative of the family to occur in western Europe. Until recently, no representative of the Urodontidae was known to occur in the British Isles, although Fowler (1891, p. 108) noted that '*Urodon rufipes* has been erroneously admitted to a place in our lists'. In 1984, however, Dr P. S. Hyman found *Bruchela rufipes* to be well established at a locality in S. Essex. The location is close to docks and industrial plant, so that the beetle may have been introduced. Six or seven species of *Bruchela* are recorded from northern and western Europe; all are associated with species or Resedaceae or Cruciferae, the known larvae feeding in the fruits.

— A small (2·1–2·8 mm), slightly elongate species. Pronotum large, slightly elongate, with the middle of the base forming a flap or shallow flange which overlaps into the base of the elytra (fig. 27). Scutellum concealed. Elytra without striae, ± parallel-sided. Head, pronotum, elytra and the clearly-exposed pygidium closely covered with fine, uniform, recumbent, greyish pubescence. Head with rostrum short, flat, the sides slightly expanded, forming a distinct ridge. Antennae arising from sides of head, reddish, short, very weakly clubbed, almost filiform (fig. 25). Eyes large, reniform, partly embracing the expanded lateral base of the rostrum. Mandibles sharply pointed, prominent. Legs with the tibiae and fore femora red to pitchy, tarsi black to pitchy, segments 1 and 2 simple, 3 bilobed, 5 long, claws appendiculate (fig. 26) . . . .**rufipes** (Olivier) (fig. 4)
> *Male with the anal segment produced at sides into a blunt tooth, easily seen in posterior or posterolateral view, centre of segment deeply excavated. Female with the anal segment simple.*
> *In waste places, on* Reseda lutea, *the larvae feeding in the fruits. A recent discovery in Britain, known from only one site in S. Essex in the London conurbation. Widely distributed throughout central and southern Europe and N. Africa.*

Family Attelabidae

This family is well defined and consists of three subfamilies which are represented in the British fauna, together with the American Pterocolinae. Several authors combine Attelabinae and Apoderinae in a single subfamily, and there is much to be said for this view, but the two subfamilies are retained in Kloet & Hincks (1977) and here.

Key to subfamilies

1   Tarsal claws separate to base (fig. 32); mandibles usually dentate externally, normally with deciduous pupal appendages; only the first two visible abdominal ventrites ± connate; inner edge of fore tibiae not dentate or asperate (fig. 33) . . . . **Rhynchitinae**
—   Tarsal claws fused at base (figs. 35, 42); mandibles not dentate on external edge, without pupal appendages; first four abdominal sternites ± connate; inner edge of fore tibiae dentate or asperate (figs. 36, 37) 2
2   Head strongly constricted at base, forming a neck which is narrower than the base of the rostrum (figs. 43, 44); pronotum strongly narrowed anteriorly, with the front margin much less than half as broad as the base; mid coxae widely separate, much further apart than fore coxae (fig. 45); elytra without a scutellary stria (fig. 46). . . . .**Apoderinae**
—   Head not constricted at base, without a neck, narrower anteriorly (at base of rostrum) than at base (figs. 38, 39); pronotum with the anterior margin much more than half as broad as basal; mid coxae scarcely more separated than fore coxae (fig. 40); elytra with a distinct scutellary stria (fig. 41). . . . . **Attelabinae**

Subfamily Attelabinae

The eastern Palaearctic is rich in species with nine genera in the subfamily, but only one of these is found in Europe, including Britain.

Genus **Attelabus** Linnaeus

The single British (and European) species is distinguished by the characters given in the subfamily key.

— A light to dark red species with strongly contrasting black legs, head, scutellum and under-side. Length 4·0–6·0 mm .... **nitens** (Scopoli)
Male with a single claw at apex of each tibia (fig. 36); rostrum narrower, longer and less strongly punctured (fig. 38). Female with two claws at the tibial apex (fig. 37); rostrum broader, shorter and more strongly punctured (fig. 39).
In oak woods and coppice, on Quercus, *less commonly on* Castanea. *The larvae in leaf rolls, especially on regrowth and 'scrub oak'. The female, having laid an egg, folds the leaf lamina, or part of it, along the line of the midrib and rolls up the double thickness of leaf. Widely distributed, but seldom abundant, throughout England and Wales and as far north as Elgin in Scotland. Less common in the north. Not recorded from Ireland. Europe southwards from southern Sweden to Siberia.*

Subfamily Apoderinae

Apoderinae, like Attelabinae, are rich in species in the eastern Palaearctic, with ten genera recognised, of which only one is found in Europe.

Genus **Apoderus** Olivier

A very distinctive genus with a single species in Britain of the two which inhabit Europe. The bell-shaped prothorax, long narrow neck, and bulging head are unmistakable.

— Characteristics as in the key to subfamilies and above. Length 5·9–8·0 mm ....
.... **coryli** (Linnaeus) (fig. 28)
Male with a single claw at the apex of each tibia (as Attelabus, *fig. 36); head narrower and less dilated at sides and dorsally (fig. 43). Female with two tibial claws apically (as* Attelabus, *fig. 37); head broader and more dilated laterally and dorsally (fig. 44).*
In woods, particularly in association with coppice. Exclusively, or almost exclusively, on Corylus avellana *in Britain, the larvae in leaf rolls. The ovipositing female makes a rather untidy roll, cutting through the midrib and rolling the leaf lamina conically across the midrib. Locally abundant throughout southern England, less common in the north and Wales, and extending into Scotland only as far as Dumfries and Roxburgh. No Irish records. All Europe to Siberia and China.*

Subfamily Rhynchitinae

This, the largest subfamily of Attelabidae, is represented in Britain by three genera, the primitive *Auletes* Schoenherr being an additional genus occurring in much of continental Europe.

Key to genera

1 Upper surface glabrous, finely pubescent only towards apex of elytra; predominantly shin-ing bright green or blue; hind coxae separated from metepisterna by abdominal lobes (fig. 47); tibiae weakly keeled on their outer edge, subcylindrical .... **Byctiscus** Thomson
— Upper surface pubescent throughout; predominantly black, blue-black or reddish, generally less brightly coloured; hind coxae reaching metepisterna, abdominal lobes wanting (fig. 34); tibiae more strongly keeled on the outer edge, often conspicuously flattened........2

2 Head constricted strongly at base (fig. 48); abdomen with the propygidium and pygidium exposed (except in male *D. mannerheimi*) (fig. 49) . . . .**Deporaus** Samouelle
— Head not constricted basally (fig. 50); abdomen with only the pygidium exposed (fig. 51) . .
. . . . **Rhynchites** Schneider

Genus **Rhynchites** Schneider

The limits of this genus have been interpreted very differently by various authors, from the extremes of Joy (1932), who included the whole subfamily, to Kloet & Hincks (1945), who recognised *Lasiorhynchites* and *Neocoenorrhinus* (as *Caenorhinus*) as distinct genera. Nor has the subgeneric classification been any more stable, with Dieckmann (1974), Hoffmann (1948), van Emden (1938) and Voss (1932), for instance, all expressing different views. Kloet & Hincks (1977) recognise three subgenera only, but the preparation of this handbook has suggested that *Pselaphorynchites* should be distinguished on taxonomic, biological and practical grounds. The treament of the sub-family thus differs from that of Dieckmann (1974) only in considering *Lasiorhynchites* as a subgenus, and in not recognising the subgenera included in his *Lasiorhynchites s. lat.*

Key to subgenera and species

1 Elytra with a distinct scutellary stria (fig. 53) 5
— Elytra with regularly-punctured striae throughout or somewhat confusedly and rugosely-punctured anteriorly, but always without a scutellary stria (fig. 52). . **(Rhynchites** s.str.) 2
2 Elytra, at least anteriorly, thickly and irregularly punctured; size larger, 4·2–9·0 mm; (species extinct in Britain) 3
— Elytra regularly punctured; size smaller, 3·0–4·5 mm 4
3 Upper surface of rostrum ± completely reddish-coppery, metallic, including the apical area from insertion of the antennae and the indistinct keel which runs from the insertion to base; size larger, 5·5–9·0 mm. . . . . **auratus** (Scopoli)
Male pronotum armed with a sharp spine anterio-laterally, directed forwards; rostrum only slightly dilated anteriad, more shining; antennae inserted in front of middle of rostrum. Female pronotum unarmed; rostrum broader anteriorly and duller; antennae inserted just behind middle of rostrum.
On Prunus, *especially* P. spinosa, *the larvae in kernels of the stones. Extinct in Britain. Formerly taken in W. Kent by Marsham, Walton and possibly others; more doubtful records from Cambridge and Dumfries. Europe, except the north, to Siberia.*
— Upper surface of rostrum black from insertion of antennae to apex and basal keel black; size smaller, 4·2–6·8 mm; pronotum of male unarmed . . . .**bacchus** (Linnaeus)
Male with rostrum only as long as, or little longer than, the head and pronotum combined, less strongly widened at apex. Female with the rostrum evidently longer than the head and pronotum combined, a little more strongly widened at apex.
On various rosaceous trees and shrubs, including Prunus, Malus *and* Crataegus, *the larvae in the fruits. Extinct in Britain. Formerly in W. Kent, E. Suffolk and Hunts. the last known specimen taken in 1843 at Birch Wood, Kent, by Standish. Europe and southern Palaearctic to W. Siberia.*
4 Upper surface entirely dark metallic red, purple, purplish-red or coppery; pubescence shorter and less outstanding, shorter than the apical tarsal segment (with claws); size larger, 4·0–5·0 mm . . . . **cupreus** (Linnaeus) (fig. 29)
Male with the rostrum shorter, about as long as the pronotum, and with the antennae inserted in front of the middle. Female rostrum longer, nearly as long as the head and pronotum together, with the antennae inserted at the mid-point.
On Sorbus aucuparia *and only rarely in Britain on other rosaceous trees and shrubs, the larvae in the fruits. Local and very patchily distributed throughout England, Wales and Scotland from N. Devon and E. Sussex to Main Argyll and Mid Perth. Western Europe to Japan, northwards to the middle of Scandinavia.*

— Upper surface entirely blue, blue-black or with a slight greenish tinge, the elytra normally bright blue, the head, pronotum and legs darker; pubescence longer and more evidently outstanding, with some setae longer than the apical tarsal segment, including claws; size smaller, 2·5–4·0 mm . . . . **caeruleus** (Degeer)

Male with the rostrum shorter, as long as, or scarcely longer than, the head. Female with the rostrum longer, as long as or longer than pronotum.

In woods and hedgerows, on rosaceous trees and shrubs, especially Crataegus *and* Prunus spinosa, *also on* Malus, Pyrus, *other species of* Prunus *and* Sorbus torminalis. *Also apparently occasionally on* Quercus. *The eggs are laid in young shoots, which the ovipositing female then partially severs, so that the larvae develop in the decaying shoot tissue, at first on the tree but then on the ground after the shoot falls off. A minor pest of fruit trees ('Twig-cutting weevil'). Locally abundant throughout England from S. Somerset eastwards and as far north as Durham, though rare in the North Midlands. Few records from Wales and not recorded from Scotland or Ireland. Europe (but not Denmark or Scandinavia), Caucasus, Iran, southern Siberia.*

5 Upper surface with fine, short, dark and closely appressed pubescence; elytra narrow, 1·5 × as long as broad *and* size small, 2·0–3·5 mm; [body dull metallic dark blue, greenish or black] . . . . (**Pselaphorynchites** Schilsky) 6
— Upper surface with long, outstanding pubescence; if elytra narrow, then size much larger, 4·0–8·5 mm 10

6 Fore tibiae without an apical tooth, simple (fig. 55) 7
— Fore tibiae with a distinct, apical, inwardly-pointing tooth (fig. 57) . . **tomentosus** Gyllenhal

Male with the mid and hind tibiae armed with an apical tooth; rostrum shorter than the pronotum, with the antennae inserted at the middle. Female with only the mid tibiae armed with an apical tooth; rostrum as long as, or longer than, the pronotum, with the antennae inserted clearly behind the middle.

On species of Salix, *(S. caprea, S. viminalis, S. repens, etc.) and* Populus, *especially P. tremula, and perhaps on other trees. The larvae in leaf buds. Local but widely distributed in England and Wales eastwards from S. Somerset and northwards to Cumberland. Recorded from only Berwick in Scotland and N. and S. Kerry in Ireland. All Europe, Anatolia, Siberia.*

7 Antennae inserted at the middle of the rostrum; rostrum as long as, or shorter than, pronotum . . . . (males) 8
— Antennae inserted behind middle of rostrum; rostrum longer than pronotum . . . (females) 9

8 Head, including eyes, broader than anterior margin of pronotum; eyes large, protuberant (fig. 54); rostrum very short, much shorter than pronotum and scarcely longer than width of head with eyes . . . . **nanus** (Paykull) (fig. 30) (see below)
— Head, including eyes, as broad as anterior margin of pronotum; eyes smaller, less protuberant (fig. 56); rostrum longer, as long as pronotum and clearly longer than the head is wide . . . . **longiceps** Thomson (see below)

9 Head, including eyes, as broad as anterior margin of elytra; rostrum evidently longer than pronotum, but not as long as head and pronotum together . . . . **nanus** (Paykull)

Differences between sexes as in the key.

On Betula, *less frequently on species of* Salix *and* Alnus, *the larvae in leaf buds. Locally abundant throughout England and Wales, though perhaps absent from Devon and Cornwall. In mainland Scotland as far north as East Ross but not recorded from the Islands. No Irish records. All Europe, Turkmenistan, Siberia.*

— Head, including eyes, narrower than anterior margin of elytra; rostrum as long as, or longer than, the head and pronotum combined . . . . **longiceps** Thomson

Sexual differences as in the key.

On Betula, Salix *and* Pyrus *species, the larvae in the leaf buds. Local. Scattered records in England from S. Hants. northwards to Cumberland but apparently absent from south-western England and Wales; however, the species was not known to be British until 1911. Scotland: W. Perth and Clyde Isles (Arran) only. No Irish records. N. and mid-Europe.*

10 Elytra narrower, 1·4–1·7 × longer than broad; rostrum shorter than, or as long as, the pronotum, straight; larger species, 4·0–8·5 mm . . . . (**Lasiorhynchites** Jekel) 11
— Elytra broader, 1·2–1·3 × longer than broad; rostrum longer than, or as long as, the pronotum, curved (scarcely so in male *pauxillus*); smaller species, 2·0–4·5 mm . . . . (**Neocoenorrhinus** Voss) 13

11 Elytral striae evanescent posteriad; larger species, 6·0–8·5 mm . . . . **cavifrons** Gyllenhal

Male with eyes larger, the head narrower and more constricted posteriad and with a

distinct impression between eyes (fig. 58), rostrum narrower, not dilated anteriad or at base and with antennae inserted at one-third from apex. Female with the eyes smaller, the head broader, less constricted posteriad and without an impression between eyes (fig. 59);rostrum expanded anteriad and basally, keeled, and with the antennae inserted in the middle.

In woods, etc., on Quercus, *the larvae in one-year-old twigs. Local and seldom abundant, but widely distributed through England from Mid-W. Yorks southwards. No records from Scotland, Wales or Ireland. Southern and mid-Europe, Asia Minor, Transcaucasus.*

—   Elytral striae continued to apex, almost equally strong throughout; smaller species, 4·0–7·5 mm 12

12   The 9th (subhumeral) elytral stria joining 10th (marginal) near its middle; colour less bright, deep blue to greenish steel-blue or blue-black; antennal segment 3 longer than 4; elytral striae and rows of interstitial punctures regular; size smaller, 4·0–6·0 mm; [resident British species] . . . .*olivaceus* Gyllenhal

Male with larger and very protuberant eyes (fig. 60); head narrower than pronotum and less rounded behind eyes; rostrum parallel-sided throughout, antennae inserted in front of middle, apex more shallowly punctured and more shining. Eyes of female smaller and less prominent (fig. 61); head as broad as pronotum and more rounded behind eyes; rostrum expanded at base and apex, antennae inserted at about middle, apex often more deeply and rugosely punctured, less shining.

In woods, on Quercus, *the larvae in one-year-old twigs. Very local. Scattered records in England from Dorset eastwards as far north as N.E. Yorks but rare in the North Midlands. Wales: Glamorgan and Monmouth. No confirmed records from Scotland. One remarkable Irish record (Armagh). Southern, western and mid-Europe.*

—   The 9th and 10th elytral striae separate throughout their length; colour brighter, rich metallic violet or peacock blue, frequently with a greenish tint anteriorly; antennal segment 3 not longer than 4; strial and interstitial punctures quasi-biseriate (displaced alternately) or confused; size larger, 5·5–7·5 mm; [doubtful or extinct British species] . . . **sericeus** Herbst

Male with the apex of the tibiae armed with a short, straight spine. Female with the tibiae unarmed.

On Quercus; *the larvae are brood-parasites in the leaf rolls of* Attelabus nitens *on oak in continental Europe, where the species is appropriately known as a 'cuckoo weevil'. Extinct in Britain, and indeed of doubtful British provenance. Seven putative British examples known, none with locality data (Allen 1964). Southern and western Europe, N. Africa; generally rare, no doubt because of its unusual life-history.*

13   At least pronotum, head and femora coppery, bronze or bronze-green, metallic; elytra reddish with legs and rostrum dark brown or black, *or* these parts concolorous with head and pronotum 17

—   Upper surface entirely black, dark blue or blue-greenish, usually with at most a slight metallic tinge; elytra not always concolorous with other parts, but never coppery, bronze or reddish 14

14   Elytra more coarsely, deeply and closely punctured, striae almost twice as broad as interstices; 9th and 10th striae (the two outermost) entire and continued to apex, or anastomosing subapically at most, not separated by an intercalary stria, or row of punctures at base (fig. 62); pronotum broadest just behind middle; femora with a coppery or greenish tinge, metallic. . . . .*aeneovirens* (Marsham) f. **fragariae** Gyllenhal (see below)

—   Elytra more finely and shallowly and less closely punctured, striae about as broad as interstices: 9th stria anastomosing with 10th at or behind middle or separated by a short intercalary stria or row of punctures at base (fig. 63); pronotum broadest at middle; femora shining black or blue-black, scarcely metallic and not coppery or greenish . . . 15

15   9th and 10th elytral striae anastomosing at middle or in apical third, without a separating intercalary stria or row of punctures at base (figs. 64, 65); pubescence of pronotum long, straight or only slightly curved, as long as or longer than first antennal segment; pubescence of elytra longer, erect, at least in part, and not uniformly directed backwards 16

—   9th and 10th elytral striae entire, continued to apex, separated at base by a short intercalary stria or row of punctures (fig. 63): pubescence of pronotum short, strongly curved and directed forwards, much shorter than length of first antennal segment; pubescence of elytra shorter, outstanding but directed obliquely backwards; [pronotum simple, elytra and pronotum usually unicolorous, black or blue-black, pronotum sometimes with a greenish metallic tinge]; length 2·1–3·1 mm . . . . **germanicus** Herbst

Male with the rostrum shorter than in the female, shorter than head and pronotum together, not dilated at apex and with the antennae inserted at about middle. Female with the rostrum as long as, or longer than, the head and pronotum together, dilated at apex and with the antennae inserted evidently behind the middle.

On a wide variety of herbaceous and shrubby Rosaceae: Fragaria, Geum, Sanguisorba, Potentilla, Rubus *and* Rosa; *also apparently on* Salix *and less frequently and certainly on* Quercus, Cornus, *etc. A pest of strawberry ('Strawberry Rhynchites'), blackberry, raspberry, loganberry, etc. The larvae in stems, flower-bearing and vegetative shoots, and stolons, which are partially detached and killed by the female after oviposition, feeding in the dying and decaying tissue. Widely distributed and common throughout England and Wales but seldom abundant, save in strawberry fields, etc. Few Scottish records except in the S.W., but extending as far north as Elgin. Throughout Ireland. All Europe, E. and mid-Asia to Siberia and Mongolia.*

16 9th stria anastomosing with 10th behind middle, at about one-quarter to one-third from apex of elytra (fig. 64); punctures of striae smaller and less strongly impressed; interstices flat, with distinct rows of small punctures; pronotum more closely punctured than head, with a narrow, shining, unpunctured, longitudinal line on disc but without small, shining areas or irregular puncturation at its sides; [upper surface dark blue or blue-black]; length 2·5–3·4 mm . . . . **interpunctatus** Stephens
        Male with the rostrum shorter, scarcely longer than the pronotum and much shorter than the head and pronotum together, antennae inserted at about middle. Female with the rostrum longer, much longer than the pronotum, as long as head and pronotum together, or nearly so, antennae inserted well behind middle.

        On Quercus. *Biology unknown or uncertain, the few published accounts almost certainly confusing* C. interpunctatus *with other species. Local but widely distributed in England from Notts. and Derby southwards; only Welsh records from Glamorgan. Not recorded from Scotland or Ireland. All Europe, Caucasus, Siberia, Algeria.*

—   9th stria anastomosing with 10th at about middle of the elytra (fig. 65); punctures of striae larger and more strongly impressed; interstices raised, with the interstitial punctures much less evident; pronotum much less closely punctured, as head, with a distinct, shallow, longitudinal furrow on disc; also with an indistinct, small, shining area on each side of disc, caused by irregularity of the puncturation; these areas joined to the basal extremity of the median furrow by an indistinct, somewhat curved sub-basal impression; [upper surface blue or dark blue]; length 2·1–3·3 mm . . . . **pauxillus** Germar
        Male with the rostrum shorter, and a little straighter, not or scarcely as long as the pronotum and only slightly longer than the width of the head across eyes, rostrum relatively a little more strongly widened at apex. Female with the rostrum longer, and more distinctly curved, as long as or longer than the pronotum and distinctly longer than the width of the head across eyes, rostrum relatively a little less strongly widened at apex.

        On a variety of rosaceous shrubs, particularly Crataegus, Prunus spinosa *and* Mespilus. *A pest of fruit trees in Europe, though not in Britain. Larvae in petioles or midveins of leaves, partially severed by the ovipositing female, which soon fall to the ground, where the larvae feed on the dying leaf tissue. Very local and uncommon, but widely distributed in England from Durham southwards, though rare in the North Midlands and not recorded from Wales or the S.W. peninsula. No reliable Scottish records; not in Ireland. Europe, Caucasus, Iran.*

17 Upper surface unicolorous coppery-bronze or bronze-green, with only tarsi and apical half of rostrum darker to black; 9th elytral stria entire to apex and anastomosing with the 10th only subapically (fig. 62); punctures of elytral striae strong and deep, about twice as broad as interstices; length 2·3–3·8 mm . . . . **aeneovirens** (Marsham)
        Male with the rostrum as long as the head and pronotum together, slightly widened at apex, and with the antennae inserted at the middle. Female with the rostrum half as long again as head and pronotum together, strongly widened at apex and with the antennae inserted well behind the middle.

        In woods, on Quercus, f. fragariae *also on* Quercus, *but stated by Hoffmann (1958) to be allotrophic and to feed also on herbaceous* Pontentilla *and* Geum. *The larvae in buds which the ovipositing female first cuts off from their sap supply by partially severing them, though they do not fall from the trees. Widely distributed and locally common in England, S. Wales and Scotland from Main Argyll and Elgin southwards, f.* fragariae *with the type form but less common. A few scattered Irish records. All Europe, Caucasus, Iran, N. Africa.*

31

—   Upper surface with the head and pronotum metallic-coppery-bronze or dark brown and the elytra a contrasting brick red, reddish-brown or orange-brown, suture usually darker, especially basally; 9th elytral stria anastomosing with 10th a little after middle, not entire to apex (fig. 66); punctures of elytral striae weak and shallow, about half as broad as interstices; length 2·7–4·5 mm. . . . . **aequatus** (Linnaeus)

Male with the rostrum as long as the head and pronotum together, apex scarcely widened. Female with the rostrum 1·3–1·4 × as long as head and pronotum together, strongly widened at apex; [antennae in both sexes inserted at about middle of rostrum].

On rosaceous trees and shrubs, chiefly Crataegus, Prunus spinosa *and* Malus, *also* Sorbus aucuparia, Mespilus, *other* Prunus *spp., etc., the larvae in the fruits. A pest of apple ('Apple Fruit Rhynchites'). Common and generally distributed throughout most of England from Durham and Mid-W. York southwards, but few records from Wales. Also recorded from Edinburgh, but absent from Ireland. Europe, northern Asia to Turkmenistan.*

Genus **Byctiscus** Thomson

About 24 species in this genus occur in the Palaearctic region but all except the two European ones occur only in eastern Asia.

Key to species

1   Apex of elytra sparsely clothed with fine, pale pubescence; underside and pygidium ± concolorous with upper surface, or not markedly darker; legs metallic, often concolorous with upper surface; head with a shallow depression between eyes in which the puncturation runs into irregular, longitudinal striations; colour shining metallic green, golden-green, blue-green, blue or violet, often with red, red-coppery or red-orange areas; size larger, 4·8–7·0 mm . . . . **betulae** (Linnaeus)

Male with a conspicuous spine on the lower margin of the pronotum in the anterior third on each side, directed forwards (fig. 67); pronotum broader and more globose; coloration normally metallic blue; antennae inserted just in front of middle of rostrum. Female with the pronotum unarmed (fig. 68); pronotum narrower and less globose; coloration normally metallic green or golden green; antennae inserted at about middle of rostrum.

On a variety of trees and shrubs, most frequently on Corylus *and* Betula *in Britain. The larvae in leaf rolls, in which the ovipositing female often incorporates several leaves, making an untidy 'cigar'. Very local and not generally common, though sometimes in numbers where found. Widely distributed in southern and midland England from Dorset eastwards and as far north as Cumberland, but records often confused with those of* Deporaus betulae. *Only one Welsh vicecounty (Glamorgan) and not recorded from Scotland or Ireland.*

—   Apex of elytra glabrous; underside and pygidium much darker than upper surface, generally a dull, metallic dark blue-black-green; coloration of legs similar; head with a deeper depression between eyes, with an impressed, narrow, longitudinal furrow in middle but puncturation distinct, not running into irregular, longitudinal striations; colour deep golden-green, much more constant than in *B. betulae*; size smaller, 4·0–5·5 mm . . . . **populi** (Linnaeus)

Differences between the sexes as in B. betulae, *except that the male rostrum is clearly longer than in the female and scarcely shorter than the pronotum (fig. 69), whereas the female rostrum is evidently shorter than the pronotum (fig. 70).*

On Populus tremula, P. alba *and possibly other trees, the larvae in leaf rolls usually constructed from a single leaf (cf.* B. betulae*). Very local, in southern England only and mainly in the east, from E. Sussex to S. Devon and N. Cornwall northwards to Worcester. Europe, western and mid-Asia to Siberia, Mongolia and northern China.*

Genus **Deporaus** Samouelle

This genus is represented by four species in two subgenera in Europe, the eastern Palaearctic fauna being much richer. Only the two species in the subgenus *Deporaus s.str.* are found in Britain.

Key to species

1 Elytra greenish-blue or blue-black, narrower, about 1·6× longer than broad (fig. 71); head with eyes fully as broad as pronotum; (propygidium in male not exposed; hind femora normal in both sexes); length 2·8–3·8 mm . . . . **mannerheimi** (Hummel)
Male with the rostrum shorter than the head, more rugose and less shining, with the apex less expanded and the antennae inserted well in front of middle; (propygidium not exposed). Female with rostrum as long as, or slightly longer than, head, much more shining and more rugose, with apex expanded and antennae inserted at, or a little behind, middle; (propygidium exposed).
On Betula, *particularly on moors and generally in wetter, more oligotrophic, areas. Biological details scanty, but larvae apparently leaf-miners in leaves which have the petioles partially gnawed through (presumably by the ovipositing female); the larvae continue their feeding in the fallen leaves. Widely but somewhat patchily distributed and often common in England, Wales and Scotland, as far north as W. Sutherland. Not recorded from Ireland. All the Palaearctic except N. Africa and the south of the Mediterranean region.*

— Elytra black, broader, about 1·4× longer than broad (fig. 72); head with eyes slightly narrower than pronotum; (propygidium of male exposed; hind femora of male strongly dilated, bulging) . . . . **betulae** (Linnaeus) (fig. 31)
Male with the hind femora strongly dilated and bulging; rostrum slightly narrower and less expanded at base. Female with the hind femora simple, not dilated; rostrum slightly broader and more expanded at base.
On Betula, Alnus, *and* Corylus, *less frequently on* Carpinus, Fagus *and other trees. Larvae in conical leaf rolls, the ovipositing female cutting across the leaf lamina and rolling the larger distal portion radially. Common and readily observed in both the adult and immature stages (leaf rolls) and widely distributed throughout the British Isles (England, Wales, Scotland and Ireland) except the Outer Hebrides, Orkney and Zetland. The commonest British attelabid. Europe, Siberia, Mongolia.*

Family Apionidae

Family status for this group has been accepted only fairly recently and some authors (e.g. Lohse, 1981; Dieckmann, 1977; Kissinger 1968; and Aslam, 1961) still regard it as a subfamily of Curculionidae. Kloet & Hincks (1977), Crowson (1967, 1956) and others are followed here in according *Apion* and its allies family rank. Crowson (1967) recognises four subfamilies (two of them British) and these are roughly the equivalents of the tribes recognised by Kissinger (1968). The latter's radical treatment of *Perapion* and other taxa (not British), which are placed in a separate tribe, Aplemonini, is not followed here.

Apart from this distinction, the subgeneric concept adopted by Kissinger for species in the exceptionally large genus *Apion*, which constitutes the bulk of the Apionidae, is closely followed. The subgenera are broadly those recognised by Wagner (1930, etc.), but Wagner's subgeneric concept was a good deal narrower than that of Kissinger (1968), Hoffmann (1958) or Kloet & Hincks (1977), and several of his subgenera are not recognised here, though they were closely followed by Dieckmann (1977).

Key to subfamilies

1 Antennae not geniculate (fig. 77); pronotum with the base not greatly broader than apex, ± parallel-sided or slightly rounded; [elytra unicolorous in most instances] . . . . . . **Apioninae**

— Antennae geniculate (fig. 78); pronotum at base twice as broad as at apex, and basal width scarcely less than that of elytra at shoulders, sides strongly convergent anteriad; [elytra with the base abruptly darker than remainder] . . . . **Nanophyinae**

Subfamily Apioninae

The subfamily is represented by a single genus, *Apion* Herbst, in Britain and Europe. The many species have a distinct general facies and various attempts to elevate subgenera or groups to the status of genera have not been universally accepted. Some of the subgenera are diagnosed by characters which are not readily observable, whilst many species are easily distinguished. The key, whilst making some use of subgeneric characters when possible, aims at being practical, and for this reason some subgenera are keyed using specific rather than subgeneric characters.

Genus **Apion** Herbst

Key to subgenera

1 Rostrum subulate, narrowed distally, wedge-shaped, with the apex at most half as broad as base, often gibbous beneath (figs. 79–86); eyes large and prominent (fig. 87); [on Papilionaceae]. . . . .**Oxystoma** Duméril
— Rostrum cylindrical or subcylindrical, ± parallel-sided, not subulate or narrowed distally, or if narrowed then apex more than half as broad as base; eyes smaller and less prominent 2
2 Upper surface of elytra (at least in part) red, yellowish, orange, reddish-brown or brown. 3
— Upper surface of elytra dark, black or blue, green or purple, sometimes with a metallic or brassy sheen but never reddish, orange or brown 5
3 Entire upper surface (except eyes and tarsal claws) red, yellowish-red or orange, legs concolorous with rest of body; pubescence sparse, even, on both pronotum and elytra, not forming any pattern; [on *Rumex* spp.]. . . . .**Apion** Herbst (s.str.)
— At least pronotum, head and rostrum dark, black or dark brown; if these parts reddish, legs much lighter; pubescence thicker, especially on thorax and shoulders of elytra, or forming elytral bands 4
4 Elytra mainly red or orange-red, rather abruptly darker (black) at base and narrowly at suture; pubescence on elytra not forming distinct bands; pronotum, head and elytra at shoulders with thick, whitish pubescence; elytra broader, less than twice as long as broad; pronotum and head black; [on Malvaceae] . . . .**Malvapion** Hoffmann
— Elytra dark red or red-brown, gradually and more obscurely darkened towards base; coloration of elytral derm somewhat obscured by pubescence, which forms three ± distinct transverse bands; elytra narrower, more than twice as long as broad; pronotum and head brown-black; [on *Urtica dioica*] . . . .**Taeniapion** Schilsky
5 Second stria of elytra united at apex to eighth; antennae inserted at base of rostrum on a strong, lateral tooth (fig. 88) *and* legs in part red; upper surface squamose, with conspicuous scales or thick pubescence (not marked in *difficile*); [on Papilionaceae] . . . . .
. . . .**Exapion** Bedel
— Second stria of elytra united at apex to ninth; if antennae inserted at base of rostrum on a lateral tooth, tooth less strong and legs entirely dark, black, blue, greenish or purple; upper surface generally not squamose, scales or thick pubescence absent. 6
6 Femora entirely, or in greater part, red, yellow or orange 7
— Femora entirely black or blue-black, or metallic blue, green or purple 10
7 Distinctly pubescent, at least ventrally and especially in the male, pubescence white, greyish-white or pale grey; elytra much less strongly arched, not forming an abrupt angle with pronotum in side view (fig. 89), wider than high when seen from behind (fig. 90) 8
— Glabrous ventrally and dorsally, or with extremely fine, hardly evident pubescence; elytra much more strongly arched, forming an abrupt and distinct angle with pronotum in side view (fig. 91), about as broad as high when seen from behind (fig. 92); [on Papilionaceae] . . . .**Protapion** Schilsky
8 Fore and mid tibiae entirely red, yellow or orange in both sexes. 9
— Fore and mid tibiae predominantly black, female with only the base of the mesothoracic tibiae obscurely and narrowly red, male with the base of both pairs of tibiae more broadly red or yellow; [on Papilionaceae] . . . .**Eutrichapion** Reitter (in part)

9   Interstices of elytra narrow, little more (1·5 ×) broad than striae; elytra narrow and sub-parallel, more than twice as long as broad, broadest at middle; size smaller, 1·8–2·4 mm; [rostrum black in both sexes; on *Mercurialis* spp.] . . . . **Kalcapion** Schilsky
—   Interstices of elytra much broader (about 3 ×) than striae; elytra more rounded at sides, not subparallel, not more than twice as long as broad, broadest just behind middle; size larger, 2·1–2·8 mm; [apex of rostrum red or yellow in male, entirely black in female; on Malvaceae]. . . . . **Pseudapion** Schilsky
10   Head between eyes with two furrows, or distinct impression, in the form of a V or U (figs. 162, 163); [pronotum finely, shallowly and distinctly punctured, shagreened between punctures; claws without teeth; base of rostrum not, or very obscurely, punctured; on Compositae] . . . . **Diplapion** Reitter
—   Head between eyes without furrows in the form of a V or U; if with an impression, this is single, longitudinal 11
11   Either with scutellum long and pointed, with two small but very distinct longitudinal carinae at base (fig. 93) *or* head between eyes with a long and deep longitudinal furrow (fig. 94); [pronotum and base of rostrum distinctly and rather closely punctured; claws toothed internally; on Malvaceae] . . . . **Aspidapion** Schilsky
—   With neither a long, pointed, carinate scutellum nor a long, deep, longitudinal furrow between eyes 12
12   Pronotum convex, somewhat globose, raised on disc and depressed at base, sides strongly rounded (figs. 183, 185, 186); [elytra short and broad, about 1·5 × as long as broad, widest behind middle; claws not toothed; on Compositae] . . . . **Omphalapion** Reitter
—   Pronotum not, or very slightly, convex; sides almost straight, parallel, subparallel or only weakly rounded. 13
13   Striae of elytra very fine, somewhat obsolete; pronotum almost impunctate, smooth; [on *Filago* and *Gnaphalium*] . . . . **Taphrotopium** Reitter
—   Striae of elytra distinct; pronotum generally punctured, rugose or shagreened 14
14   Rostrum with a conspicuous tooth or dentiform process on each side at base (which is not, however, as strong as in *Exapion* — see couplet 5) on which the antennae are inserted (fig. 95); [on Compositae] . . . . **Ceratopion** Schilsky
—   Rostrum simple at base, only slightly thickened or angled at insertion of the antennae . . 15
15   Antennae with segments broader; first segment (scape) markedly conical, at apex broader than fore tibia at its narrowest part; second segment (first funicular) very abruptly thick-ened from a narrow base (best seen in oblique lateral view) (fig. 96); segments 3–8 globose, ± quadrate; pronotum very coarsely punctured, with a broad, deep furrow at base (fig. 97); [on Compositae] . . . . **Ceratapion** Schilsky (in part)
—   Antennal segments narrower; if scape conical, less markedly so and apex narrower than fore tibia at its narrowest part; first funicular segment only gradually thickened from base (fig. 98); segments 3–8 variable, but some usually elongate; pronotum less coarsely punctured 16
16   Sutural striae prolonged to the base of the elytra; pronotum conspicuously contracted just in front of base and less so just behind apex, sides bisinuate (fig. 100); [antennae inserted in basal quarter of rostrum; size small, 1·1–2·3 mm; on Labiatae] . . . . . . **Thymapion** Deville
—   Sutural striae not prolonged to base of elytra, normally not, or scarcely, passing apex of scutellum; if pronotum contracted sub-basally then less conspicuously so and sides only weakly bisinuate; [antennae often inserted in front of basal quarter of rostrum; frequently longer than 2·3 mm] 17
17   Scutellum invisible or extremely small (fig. 101); pronotum diffusely, finely and shallowly punctured, elongate, broadest slightly in front of middle, somewhat angled at sides (fig. 102); [elytra ovoid, without obvious shoulders (fig. 101), broadest in middle; on Papilionaceae] . . . . **Synapion** Schilsky
—   Scutellum normal, distinctly visible from above; pronotum more strongly punctured, less elongate and not angled at sides. 18
18   Elytra markedly dilated posteriorly, broadest behind middle, pear-shaped, less than 1·5 × longer than broad, little broader at base than pronotum, shoulders weakly developed (fig. 99); [on Papilionaceae, Genisteae] . . . . **Pirapion** Reitter
—   Elytra rounded at sides, not dilated behind, broadest at about middle, broader at base than pronotum, shoulders more strongly developed 19
19   Rostrum straight or only weakly curved, usually short and broad; generally more depressed species, elytra clearly broader than high; tarsal claws not toothed internally (weakly so in

A. *sedi*); [on Polygonaceae, Crassulaceae and Plumbaginaceae] . . . . . . **Perapion** Wagner

— Rostrum strongly curved, usually long and slender; often less depressed species, elytra as high as broad, higher than broad, or little broader than high; tarsal claws toothed internally; [on Papilionaceae, *Betula* or *Salix*] 20

20 Orbit of eyes ventrally, and meso- and metathoracic epimera, with conspicuous white setae; antennae entirely dark; eyes not protuberant; [head shagreened between eyes, without striations; sometimes with a bronze or brassy reflection; on *Betula*] . .**Trichapion** Wagner

— Without this combination of characters. If orbit of eyes ventrally, and meso- and metathoracic epimera, with conspicuous white setae then at least proximal segments of antennae yellow to red and eyes protuberant; [elytra seldom with a bronze or brassy sheen; though sometimes blue or green; not normally on *Betula*] 21

21 Elytra more convex, especially evident in profile, the elytra conspicuously angled with pronotum (fig. 91); [pronotum narrow, scarcely half as broad as elytra; legs comparatively long and slender] . . . . **Protapion** Schilsky (in part)

— Elytra less convex, not conspicuously angled with pronotum, but making a $\pm$ smooth outline in profile (as fig. 89); [pronotum often broader compared with elytra; legs more robust] 22

22 Elytra oval, broadest at middle, or even slightly in front of middle (figs. 103, 104); [size small, 1·5–2·3 mm; on *Trifolium* spp.] . . . .**Catapion** Schilsky

— Elytra broadest behind middle (fig. 105); [size often larger, to 3·2 mm; not normally on *Trifolium* spp. (with the exception of *A. virens*)] 23

23 Elytral interstices as narrow as, or narrower than, the striae (best seen with the light coming from the side) (fig. 106); [small species, 1·7–2·2 mm; entirely black, on *Salix* spp.] . . . .
. . . .**Melanapion** Wagner

— Elytral interstices broader than striae; [often larger species, to 3·2 mm; often blue, blue-black or green (but including all-black species); on Papilionaceae] 24

24 Upper surface completely, or almost completely, glabrous (at least rostrum, disc of pronotum and disc of elytra without pubescence; very fine setae sometimes discernible at sides of elytra); [elytra always blue, green, blue-black or bluish-violet; size moderately large, 1·9–3·2 mm; elytra short-oval, never more than 1·5 × longer than broad] . . . .
. . . . **Pseudotrichapion** Wagner

— Upper surface distinctly pubescent, sometimes finely and sparsely so, but setae evident on rostrum, disc of pronotum and disc of elytra as well as their sides; [elytra variously coloured — black in some species; size on average smaller, 1·6–2·9 mm; elytra of various shapes, including long-oval in several species] . . . .**Eutrichapion** Reitter

Subgenus **Perapion**

As recognised here, this subgenus contains about 30 species in Europe, of which eight are British.

Key to species

1 Colour of elytra rich reddish-purple or purple; pronotum purple with a golden or bronzy sheen; elytra at base bordered, i.e. with a raised edge or keel, from the scutellum evanescent at about the 4th stria, suture slightly raised basad (fig. 107); pronotum parallel-sided, elongate; size larger, 2·8–4·0 mm; [pronotum with a deep sub-basal depression which does not run into a longitudinal stria; sparsely punctured, strongly shagreened between punctures; on *Limonium* spp.] . . . .**limonii** Kirby

Secondary sexual differences slight. Male with rostrum slightly shorter, about 2·6 × longer than basal width, and with the antennae a little nearer middle. Female with rostrum longer, about 2·8–3·0 × longer than broad and with the antennae inserted a little more behind middle.

In saltmarshes, most frequently on Limonium vulgare *but also on* L. bellidifolium; *less commonly on cliffs, on* L. binervosum; *the larvae probably in rootstocks. Locally abundant from Dorset and Isle of Wight eastwards round the coast to W. Norfolk. Not in northern or western England, Wales, Scotland or Ireland. Restricted to coasts of the Atlantic and Mediterranean in Western Europe.*

—   Colour of elytra black, blue, blue-black or slightly greenish or brassy but never purple; pronotum without a golden or bronzy sheen; elytra without a basal border between scutellum and 4th stria and not raised basally at suture; pronotum rounded at sides, or if parallel-sided, less elongate; size smaller, 1·6–3·5 mm; [on Polygonaceae and Crassulaceae, not on *Limonium*]. 2

2   Elytra blue, dark blue, greenish-blue or slightly violet, bronze or brassy, often metallic but always contrasting with the black pronotum 3

—   Elytra entirely black, concolorous with the pronotum (and other parts of the body) 8

3   Elytra more elongate, 1·5–1·6 × longer than broad; scutellum elongate; size larger, 2·6–3·5 mm; pronotum quadrate or slightly elongate, less rounded at sides; [first segment of hind tarsi of male with a distinct tooth, visible in oblique view (fig. 108); generally on species of *Rumex (Rumex)*] 4

—   Elytra less elongate, 1·2–1·4 × longer than broad; scutellum about as long as broad; size smaller, 1·6–2·4 mm; pronotum transverse, more rounded at sides; [hind tarsi of male unarmed; on species of *Rumex (Acetosella)* and *R. (Acetosa)*] 7

4   First segment of hind tarsi with a distinct tooth or spur which projects inwards and downwards (fig. 108) and is thus best seen in oblique view*; rostrum shorter, never longer than pronotum, and closely punctured almost to apex, dull in front of the antennal insertion; antennae inserted just behind middle of rostrum. . . . .(males) 5

—   First segment of hind tarsi simple, unarmed (fig. 109); rostrum long, often longer than pronotum, and more diffusely punctured in front of the antennal insertion, shining, at least in part; antennae inserted at about one-third from base of rostrum . . . . . (females) 6

5   Rostrum shorter, straight, about as long as head, about 2·5 × longer than basal width, distinctly and gradually narrowed from base to apex, wedge-shaped (fig. 110); elytra more shining, microsculpture slightly coarser. Length 2·8–3·1 mm . . . .**hydrolapathi** (Marsham) (fig. 73) (see below)

—   Rostrum longer, slightly curved, longer than head, more than 2·5 × longer than basal width, cylindrical, of equal width throughout (fig. 112); elytra duller, microsculpture finer. Length 2·6–3·5 mm. . . . . **violaceum** Kirby (see below)

6   Rostrum shorter, at most as long as, or little longer than, the pronotum, distinctly narrowed apically from insertion of the antennae (fig. 111), straight or very slightly curved; elytra more shining, microsculpture coarser (as male). Length 2·8–3·1 mm. . . . . **hydrolapathi** (Marsham)
     Sexual differences as in key.
     On species of Rumex *subgenus* Rumex *('Docks'), by no means restricted to* R. *hydrolapathum, but also on* R. obtusifolium, R. crispus, *etc. Larvae in the stems. Common throughout England and Wales; apparently more local in Scotland, as far north as Easterness. Common over the whole of Ireland. Remarkable as an almost entirely coastal species throughout the rest of Europe.*

—   Rostrum longer, always longer than the pronotum, cylindrical, as broad at apex as at base, slightly expanded at insertion of antennae and sometimes also a little before apex (fig. 113), clearly curved; elytra duller, microsculpture finer (as male). Length 2·6–3·5 mm. . . . . **violaceum** Kirby
     Sexual differences as in key.
     On a wide variety of species of Rumex (Rumex) *and* R. (Acetosa), *having a wider range of hosts than* A. hydrolapathi, *and probably occurring on most species of 'docks' as well as* R. (A.) acetosa. *Larvae in the stems. Common and abundant throughout the British Isles, including Orkney and Zetland, though under-recorded in much of Scotland and Ireland.*

7   Underside of head with large, deep punctures on either side of the median punctured depression (fig. 114); vertex and pronotum more closely and deeply punctured, the pronotal interspaces narrower than the punctures (fig. 115); elytra broader, about 1·2–1·3 × longer than broad; [colour usually dark blue-black]. Length 1·9–2·4 mm. . . . . **affine** Kirby
     Male with the rostrum shorter, about as long as pronotum, and with the antennae inserted at a little in front of middle. Female with the rostrum longer than the pronotum and with the antennae inserted at the mid-point.
     Probably on Rumex acetosa *and possibly also* R. acetosella; *the larvae are reported to inhabit galls in the inflorescences, but biological details are scanty, particularly for British*

*It is sometimes erroneously stated that the males of *A. (P.) hydrolapathi* lack this tooth

material. Local and not generally common, but widely distributed throughout England, though not recorded from a large block of southern counties. Only Dumfries and Wigtown in Scotland, S. Kerry in Ireland, and not recorded from Wales. Palaearctic.

— Underside of head unpunctured on either side of the median depression, transversely striate (fig. 116); vertex and pronotum less closely and more shallowly punctured, the pronotal interspaces as broad as, or broader than, the punctures (fig. 117); elytra narrower, about 1·3–1·4 × longer than broad; [colour often brighter, blue-black or violet-blue]. Length 1·6–2·3 mm . . . . **marchicum** Herbst

Secondary sexual differences as in A. affine *(above), though rostrum a little longer and straighter (in both sexes).*

On Rumex acetosella *agg., the larvae in complex galls on the roots or rootstocks. Somewhat local, but generally common throughout the British Isles as far north as Caithness, but not in the Outer Hebrides, Orkney or Zetland, and less common in Scotland generally. All Europe except the south-east.*

8 Scutellum small, transverse to quadrate, not sulcate (fig. 118); head distinctly punctured, punctures occasionally running into a single stria between eyes but interocular area never completely striated; puncturation of pronotum less close and deep, at least some interspaces broader than punctures and often with a median unpunctured area; pubescence less distinct; usually more elongate, elytra twice as long as broad, and smaller; length 1·7–2·4 mm; tarsal claws weakly toothed internally (fig. 119). [On Crassulaceae] . . . .**sedi** Germar

Male with the first segment of each tarsus armed internally with a small but distinct tooth, most easily seen on the hind tarsi; rostrum shorter, shorter than, or about as long as, the pronotum, with the apex duller and the antennae inserted at about middle. Female with the tarsi simple, unarmed; rostrum longer, as long as, or longer than, pronotum, with apex more shining and the antennae inserted well behind the middle.

On Crassulaceae, *principally on* Sedum acre *and* S. anglicum *in Britain, but possibly also on other* Sedum *and* Sempervivum *species. Larvae in mines, at first in leaves then later in stems. Very local, but well scattered in England from W. Cornwall to W. Norfolk, chiefly on the coast. More isolated records from Glamorgan, S. Lancaster, Ayr and the Isle of Man. Not in Ireland.*

— Scutellum longer, elongate, with a central groove, furrow or sulcus (fig. 120); head clearly striated between eyes; puncturation of pronotum closer and deeper, interspaces more generally narrower than punctures and without a median unpunctured area; pubescence more distinct; usually less elongate, elytra about 1·8 × longer than broad, and larger; length 2·2–2·8 mm; tarsal claws simple (fig. 121); [on Polygonaceae] 9

9 More thickly pubescent, especially along the outermost elytral interstice and the thoracic episterna, where the pubescence is so thick as to obscure the dermal colour; pubescence slightly golden; scutellar sulcus stronger; pronotum more shining, with the puncturation close and finer; tarsi longer and more slender; [male with the hind tarsi unarmed; penis shorter, subulate (fig. 123); on *Polygonum*] . . . . **lemoroi** Brisout

Male with the rostrum shorter, not as long as the pronotum. Female with the rostrum longer, about as long as the pronotum.

On Polygonum aviculare, *the larvae in stems; apparently there are two generations a year. Rare and very local; E. Kent, Surrey and Cambridge only, but probably little looked-for since its discovery in Britain (Easton 1946).*

— Less thickly pubescent, and not more so on the outermost elytral interstice or the thoracic episterna; never obscuring the dermal colour; pubescence whitish; scutellar sulcus weaker, pronotum duller, with the puncturation less close but coarser; tarsi shorter and more robust; [male with the first segment of the hind tarsi armed internally with a distinct tooth; penis longer, simply rounded at apex (fig. 122); on *Rumex*] . . . . **curtirostre** Germar (fig. 74)

Male with hind tarsi as key above; rostrum shorter, as long as, or little longer than, the head. Female with the hind tarsi simple; rostrum longer, distinctly longer than head. Antennae inserted near the middle of rostrum in both sexes.

On a wide variety of Rumex *species, including members from each of the three subgenera:* Rumex s.str., Acetosa *and* Acetosella. *Exact range of hostplants not known in Britain. Larvae in stems. Very common and abundant throughout England, Wales and Scotland to Orkney (not recorded from Zetland). Abundant and widespread in Ireland. All Europe and Asia to Japan.*

Subgenus **Malvapion**

This is a small subgenus which contains only the one very distinctive species in Europe. It is immediately recognisable by the reddish-yellow elytra, which have a black or dark base.

— Length 1·8–2·4 mm...**malvae** Fabricius
Male with the rostrum shorter, shorter than the pronotum, and pubescent almost to apex; middle and hind tibiae with weak apical teeth. Female with the rostrum longer, as long as, or slightly longer than, the pronotum, pubescent only to insertion of antennae, or not much further, apex shining; tibiae unarmed.
On Malvaceae, particularly Malva sylvestris, and hence frequently on roadside verges, waste places, and near the sea. Larvae in the fruits. Locally abundant in southern and midland England, as far north as Leicester and Derby, but absent from Scotland and Ireland and recorded in Wales only from Glamorgan. All the Palaearctic except the north.

Subgenus **Pseudapion**

Only one of the three European species of this Palaearctic subgenus occurs in Britain.

— Length 2·1–2·8 mm.. **rufirostre** (Fabricius)
Male with the rostrum shorter, a little longer than the pronotum, and yellow to yellowish-red from insertion of the antennae to apex; fore coxae and antennae entirely clear yellow. Female with the rostrum longer, as long as pronotum and head together, entirely black; fore coxae black, antennae reddish, darker, especially club.
On Malva sylvestris and M. neglecta on roadsides, waste places, etc. Larvae in fruits. Generally common and locally abundant in southern England as far north as Durham and the Isle of Man, but rarer in the north. Very local in Ireland, recorded from four or five vice-counties. Not in Scotland and recorded in Wales only from Glamorgan. Europe, North Africa, Asia Minor, etc.

Subgenus **Aspidapion**

Three of the four European species of this subgenus inhabit Britain, one being a recent discovery. Other species are known from Madagascar (Kissinger, 1968), the Caucasus and the Oriental region.

Key to species

1 Head between eyes with at most a shallow, narrow stria, or confluent punctures forming a line, never with a deep furrow; elytral striae well-marked, interstices narrower, about 3 × broader than striae; rounded, less distinctly shining, black; scutellum longer and triangular, about $2\frac{1}{2}$ × longer than basal width, bearing two distinct, longitudinal carinae at base (fig. 93). Length 2·5–3·3 mm 2
— Head between eyes with a large, deep and very distinct longitudinal furrow which is shorter than the length of the eyes (fig. 94); elytral striae fine, but distinct, interstices very wide and flat, about 5 × broader than striae, shining aeneous or brassy; scutellum elongate but shorter, about twice as long as broad, simple at base. Length 2·9–3·6 mm ....
....**aeneum** (Fabricius)
Male with fore tibiae strongly bent inwards (fig. 124); all tibiae armed with an apical hook; rostrum slightly shorter and broader, the antennae inserted at about one-third from base. Female with fore tibiae straight (fig. 125); all tibiae unarmed; rostrum slightly longer and narrower, the antennae inserted at about one-quarter from base.
Chiefly on Malva sylvestris but probably also on other Malvaceae, the larvae in the stems. Generally common and locally abundant throughout England and in Scotland as far north as

the Lothians. *Recorded only from Glamorgan in Wales. Very local and not common in Ireland. Palaearctic region.*

2   Fore tibia distinctly inward-curving at apex, with a conspicuous, pointed tooth or hook apically (*cf.* fig. 126); rostrum shorter, straighter and duller, as long as, or only a little longer than, the pronotum; antennae inserted less closely to head, about two-thirds from apex of rostrum; ....(males) 3

—   Fore tibia with the inner margin more or less straight, not distinctly inward-curving at apex, and without an apical tooth or hook (as *A. aeneum*, fig. 125); rostrum longer, much more curved, and more shining, distinctly longer than the pronotum to as long as the pronotum and head together; antennae inserted nearer head, about three-quarters from apex of rostrum; .... (females) 4

3   Upper surface more strongly shining, elytra distinctly shining, pronotum less dull, the punctures shallower and less close, interspaces about as broad as punctures, shagreened but slightly shining; rostrum a little longer, just longer than the pronotum, and less thickly punctured; head flat or slightly raised between eyes, strongly punctured but somewhat shining; penis bluntly rounded at apex, without subapical dorsal projections or apical knob (fig. 127), weakly curved in side view (fig. 128); average size larger, 2·7–3·1 mm; (on Malvaceae other than *Althea officinalis*, especially *Malva sylvestris*)...................
....**radiolus** (Marsham) (see below)

—   Upper surface duller, less strongly shining; elytra only weakly shining, pronotum much duller, the punctures deeper and closer, interspaces narrower than punctures, strongly shagreened and dull; rostrum slightly shorter, as long as pronotum, and more thickly and strongly punctured; head with a slight depression between eyes, strongly punctured and dull; penis narrowed and strongly produced distad, with a distinct knob or small spherical swelling at apex (fig. 129), strongly curved in side view and with distinct subapical dorsal projections (visible in side view) (fig. 130); average size smaller, 2·5–2·9 mm); (on *Althea officinalis*) ....**soror** Rey (see below)

4   Rostrum strongly curved, longer, about as long as the pronotum and head together, widened basad and distad, distinctly narrowed in the middle, finely and remotely punctured, strongly shining; pronotum less closely and more shallowly punctured, somewhat shining; upper surface generally rather more shining; scutellum narrower, more pointed at apex, with the tip less clearly raised; size on average a little larger, 2·7–3·3 mm; (on Malvaceae other than *Althea officinalis*)................................. **radiolus** (Marsham)
Sexual differences as in key.
On a wide variety of Malvaceae; particularly on Malva sylvestris *but also on* M. neglecta*, possibly other species of* Malva, Althea rosea *(in gardens) and species of* Lavatera. *Larvae in stems. Common and locally abundant throughout England and Wales (the commonest of the Mallow Apion). Local in Scotland as far north as Stirling. Scattered records throughout Ireland, but not very common. Palaearctic region.*

—   Rostrum rather more strongly curved, shorter, not as long as the pronotum and head together, much less strongly widened basad and distad, only slightly narrowed in the middle, sides subparallel throughout, much more strongly and closely punctured, much duller; upper surface generally rather less shining; scutellum broader, more rounded at apex, generally with the tip more obviously raised; size on average a little smaller, 2·8–3·0 mm; (on *Althea officinalis*) .... **soror** Rey
Sexual differences as in key.
On Althea officinalis, *and only on this host (but information very limited). A recent discovery, having been confused previously with* A. (Aspidapion) radiolus. *Larvae in the stems. Known from Burham Marsh, E. Kent, and Camber, E. Sussex, but likely to be more widespread. Distribution in Europe not accurately known, but recorded from southern and western France and probably widespread.* Althea officinalis *occurs throughout Europe, except the north, and there are many continental records of* A. radiolus *on the plant.*

Subgenus **Taeniapion**

This subgenus comprises several Palaearctic and Afrotropical species, of which three occur in Europe but only one in Britain.

Our species has elytra which are, at least in part, dark red or reddish-brown, with dense pubescence forming a pattern of three ± distinct transverse bands. The elytra are narrow, almost parallel-sided. The tarsal claws are not toothed internally.

— Length 1·9–2·3 mm . . . . **urticarium** (Herbst)
Male with the rostrum shorter, as long as, or shorter than, the pronotum, pubescent almost to apex. Female with the rostrum longer, longer than pronotum, and glabrous from insertion of antennae to apex.
On Urtica dioica: *also, according to Fowler (1891), on* U. urens *(but on the continent of Europe* A. (T.) rufulum *Wencker replaces* A. urticarium *on this host). Larvae in stems at the nodes. Local, but abundant where found, throughout southern England as far north as Hereford, Hunts and Leicester. Only Welsh records from Glamorgan. Not in Ireland or Scotland. Europe to eastern Asia.*

Subgenus **Kalcapion**

This subgenus contains three species of which two occur in Britain; all feed in the stems of *Mercurialis* spp. as larvae.

Key to species

1   Upper surface with uniform, sparse, white pubescence, third elytral interstice at base with at most a very few extra setae, without an obvious little patch of pubescence; tarsi and extreme apex of tibiae dark brown to black; antennae mostly dark to black with only the first segment obscurely reddish; [on *Mercurialis perennis*]. Length 2·0–2·4 mm . . . .
. . . . **pallipes** Kirby
Male with the rostrum shorter, about as long as pronotum, shining but with sparse pubescence to apex; antennae inserted at about one-third from base. Female with the rostrum longer, distinctly longer than the pronotum, very shining and without a trace of pubescence between antennal insertion and apex, antennae inserted at about one-quarter from base.
On Mercurialis perennis *in woods, etc.; particularly on basic soils. Larvae in stems. Common, but somewhat patchily distributed, throughout England and Wales and in Scotland as far north as the Lothians. A single record from Down in Ireland, where the foodplant is rare. Europe and the Caucasus.*
—   Upper surface with rather more distinct pubescence which is replaced on the disc of the elytra by finer, darker setae, giving the impression of a distinct bare patch, especially evident behind; third elytral interstice at base with a short, longitudinal patch of denser pubescence; tibiae entirely, and tarsi predominantly, yellow or yellowish-red; claws, and sometimes the apices of the tarsal segments, obscurely darker to black; antennae except club reddish; [on *Mercurialis anua*]. Length 1·8–2·4 mm . . . . **semivittatum** Gyllenhal
Secondary sexual differences much as A. (K.) pallipes *(above), but antennae inserted slightly closer to base of rostrum in both sexes.*
On Mercurialis annua *in waste places, etc. Larvae at nodes in stems. Extremely local, though plentiful where it occurs, in England not recorded outside the south (E. and W. Kent, E. Sussex, S. Essex and Wilts.). Not in Wales, Scotland or Ireland. Central and southern Europe as far north as the Netherlands and the German Rhineland; Azores, Canaries and N. Africa.*

Subgenus **Exapion**

This subgenus has about 30 species in Europe and is also represented in the Afro-tropical region, but only four species are found in Britain.

Key to species

1   Upper surface uniformly pubescent, the scales or setae of the same size and colour throughout, with no tendency to form a pattern except that the elytral striae are frequently evident

41

through the pubescence (which may also be partially abraded in old weevils); occasionally the pubescence is slightly denser at the scutellum and base of the third interstice; pubescence of pronotum not, or only slightly and gradually, denser at sides than on disc 2

— Upper surface with unequally-distributed pubescence which is not of uniform colour but varies from white through yellowish to brown, the broader, whitish scales forming a pattern of longitudinal bands or stripes on the elytra, either completely covering the third to fifth interstices from base to apex or incomplete and oblique from the shoulders inwards to about a half to one-third from apex and again obscurely underneath at apex; pubescence of pronotum distinctly and rather abruptly denser at sides than on disc . . . 3

2 Pronotum and elytra densely clothed with white or greyish-white scales which obscure the dermal microsculpture; tibiae, and especially femora, obscurely darker in part, not clear reddish-yellow; rostrum longer, in the female much longer than the head and pronotum together; [on *Ulex*]. Length 1·9–2·5 mm . . . . **ulicis** (Forster) (fig. 75)

Male with the rostrum shorter, about as long as the pronotum and shorter than the antennae; antennae much shorter, segments 3 and 4 less than twice as long as broad; first segment of hind tarsi angled internally, though not developed as a strong tooth (fig. 131). Female with the rostrum very long, much longer than the head and pronotum together and longer than the antennae (fig. 88); antennae longer, segments 3 and 4 more than twice (3–4 ×) as long as broad; first segment of hind tarsi simple.

On Ulex europaeus *and probably on other* Ulex *species. Larvae in pods, several individuals to a pod. Common and very abundant throughout England and Wales and in Scotland as far north as E. Ross, but becoming scarcer in the north and not recorded from the Outer Hebrides, Orkney or Zetland. Generally common in Ireland as far north as Roscommon and Monaghan but not recorded from northern Ulster. Western Europe including northern Spain and Portugal but replaced in southern Spain and N. Africa by other species.*

— Pronotum and elytra rather sparsely clothed with narrow, whitish pubescence through which details of the dermal microsculpture may be clearly seen; tibiae and femora clear yellowish-red, not darkened; rostrum shorter, not, or only slightly, longer than the pronotum in either sex; [on *Genista tinctoria*]. Length 2·0–2·3 mm . . . .**difficile** Herbst

Male with first segment of hind (and middle) tarsi armed with a conspicuous, curved spur or hook (fig. 132); rostrum short, shorter than the pronotum. Female with hind tarsi unarmed; rostrum longer, about as long as pronotum.

On Genista, *in Britain chiefly or exclusively on* G. tinctoria. *Larvae in pods, one or two (occasionally three) to a pod. Very local and scarce; Isle of Wight, Dorset, S. Hants, E. Sussex, W. Kent, Surrey, E. Gloucester and Worcester. Not recorded from northern England, Wales, Scotland or Ireland. Europe as far north as Denmark.*

3 Longitudinal bands of pubescence on elytra incomplete and oblique, running from the shoulders inwards to the third interstice and interrupted at about one-half to one-third from apex; elytra longer, narrower and higher, almost parallel-sided and higher than broad when viewed from behind; pronotum elongate or quadrate; legs longer; [male hind tarsal hook large and conspicuous; on *Cytisus*]. Length 2·4–3·0 mm . . . . **fuscirostre** (Fabricius)

Male with a strong, curved spur on the first segment of the hind tarsi (fig. 133); claw joint of fore tarsi with a blunt tooth at base; fore claws long and weakly curved; rostrum shorter, about as long as pronotum. Female with the tarsi unarmed; claw joint of fore tarsi unarmed; fore claws shorter and more strongly curved; rostrum longer, as long as, or little shorter than, head and pronotum together.

Exclusively on Cytisus scoparius, *the larvae in the pods. Somewhat local but generally common in south-east and central southern England as far west as Dorset and northwards to Salop, Radnor and E. and W. Norfolk. Absent from much of south-west England and not in the north, Scotland (dubious records only) or Ireland. Europe northwards to southern Sweden; N. Africa.*

— Longitudinal bands of pubescence on elytra complete and straight, covering the third to fifth interstices; elytra shorter, broader, more rounded at sides and more depressed, as broad as, or broader than, high when viewed from behind; pronotum transverse; legs shorter; [male hind tarsi unarmed (fig. 134); on *Genista*]. Length 2·2–2·5 mm . . . . .**genistae** Kirby

Male with the rostrum shorter and straighter, about as long as the head and pronotum together. Female with the rostrum longer and more curved, evidently longer than the head and pronotum together.

On Genista, *chiefly, if not exclusively in Britain, on* G. anglica *and so mainly in moors and bogs. Larvae in the pods. Very local and sporadic, but widely distributed, from Dorset*

eastwards through southern England to Elgin. Absent from Wales and Ireland and from many vice-counties in the rest of Britain. A very narrow, Atlantic, distribution in Europe, being known from France, Portugal and northern Spain besides Great Britain.

Subgenus **Apion** s.str.

The name *Erythrapion* Schilsky is the more familiar one for the distinctive 'red' *Apion* species, but the correct subgeneric name for the group is *Apion* s.str, (Kissinger 1968). The nomenclature of the species has long differed in the traditions of Britain and other parts of Europe. Here, the usage established by Thompson and Alonso Zarazaga (1988) is followed. Accordingly, the appropriate changes have been made, although they are bound to cause confusion, particularly as the name *frumentarium* must be transferred to the species long known as *miniatum*. The subgenus contains 14 species and is restricted to the Palaearctic. All five species occurring in western Europe are found in the British Isles.

Key to species

1 Sides and undersurface of head between eyes and pronotum ('temples') punctured throughout, the punctures being somewhat less close basad (fig. 135); larger species, length 2·7–4·4 mm; [on species of *Rumex (Rumex)* and *R. (Acetosa)*] 2

— Sides and undersurface of head punctured immediately behind eyes but with a wide, un-punctured area basally which is finely striated transversely (fig. 139); smaller species, length 1·9–3·2 mm [on *Rumex (Acetosella) acetosella* agg.] 3

2 Head long and narrowed anteriorly before eyes, temples twice as long as the width of an eye and at least $1\frac{1}{2}\times$ as long as its length (fig. 136); eyes smaller, more prominent; pronotum more strongly rounded at sides and with a distinct median longitudinal stria at base; larger, length 3·6–4·4 mm; [male with the penis massive (fig. 138), compressed except at apex, which is greatly dilated, fan-shaped (fig. 137); on species of *Rumex (Rumex)*] . . . . .
. . . . **frumentarium** (Linnaeus)
 Male with the rostrum broader and straighter, broadest subapically, with the apical half duller. Female with the rostrum narrower and more curved, broadest at antennal insertion and with the apical half more shining.
 On broad-leaved docks, Rumex obtusifolius, R. crispus, R. hydrolapathum, R. con-glomeratus, *etc. Larvae in stems, rootstocks and petiole bases. Widely distributed and generally common throughout England and Wales. Dumfries, Kirkcudbright, Dunbarton; other Scottish records requiring confirmation. Widespread in Ireland. Europe eastwards to mid-Asia.*

— Head much shorter, not narrowed in front, temples little longer than either the width or length of an eye (fig. 143); eyes larger and less prominent; pronotum less rounded at sides, particularly in the male, and with a round depression at base, at most with a very obscure and faint stria; smaller, length 2·7–3·3 mm; [male with the penis slender (fig. 145); apex finely acuminate (fig. 144); predominantly on *Rumex (Acetosa) acetosa*]. . . . .
. . . .**cruentatum** Walton
 Male with the rostrum slightly shorter, thicker, straighter and duller, about as long as head; antennae inserted just behind middle. Female rostrum longer, thinner, more curved and shining, longer than the head; antennae inserted at about one-third from base.
 On Rumex acetosa *and, on the continent, other* Rumex *species, including* R. acetosella. *Larvae in lower stems and also roots. Rather local but widely distributed throughout England, Wales and Ireland. Less common in Scotland, to N. Aberdeen and the Outer Hebrides. Europe, Asia Minor.*

3 Pronotum transverse; elytra narrow, almost parallel-sided and up to $3\times$ as long as the pronotum (fig. 146); pubescence sparser, particularly beneath; head slightly transverse; [smaller, on average, length 1.9–2.5 mm] . . . . **rubens** Stephens*

*Dieckmann (1977) gives Walton (1844) as the author of this name, showing that the name does not appear in Stephens (1831), but having apparently overlooked Stephens (1839).

43

Male with the rostrum little longer than the head, pubescent and dull almost to apex, straighter. Female with the rostrum as long as pronotum, glabrous and shining in the apical half, more strongly curved.

In sandy places on Rumex acetosella *agg., the larvae in galls on the petioles and midribs. Local, but widely distributed throughout England and Wales. Scotland: Kirkcudbright and Fife. Ireland: E. Cork, Wexford, Wicklow, Dublin. Europe, Siberia, mid-Asia, N. Africa.*

— Pronotum quadrate to elongate; elytra broader, rounded at sides, not more than 2.5 × longer than pronotum (fig. 140); pubescence denser; head longer than broad; [larger, on average, length 2.1–3.2 mm] 4

4 Rostrum almost straight, in male as long as, or nearly as long as, pronotum (fig. 147); in female as long as, or slightly longer than, pronotum (fig. 148); elytra less rounded at sides, broadest at middle; [length 2·2–3·2 mm] . . . . **rubiginosum** Grill
Male with the rostrum shorter, broader and duller than in the female (see key).

In sandy places on Rumex acetosella *agg., the larvae in root galls. Very local and not generally common, but widely distributed throughout England and Wales as far north as Westmorland. Not recorded from Scotland or Ireland. Europe, N. Africa, W. and mid-Asia.*

— Rostrum curved, shorter than the pronotum in both sexes (figs. 141, 142); elytra more rounded at sides, broadest just behind middle; [length 2·1–2·8 mm] . . .**haematodes** Kirby
Male with the rostrum shorter than the head (fig. 141) and slightly broader and duller. Female with the rostrum as long as, or longer than, the head (fig. 142) and narrower and more shining.

On Rumex acetosella *agg. in arenaceous and dry, peaty areas, the larvae in rootstocks. Common and abundant throughout the British Isles, including the Outer Hebrides, Orkney and Zetland. By far the commonest 'red' species on* Rumex acetosella. *Europe, N. Africa, Asia Minor.*

Subgenus **Thymapion**

Only four of the dozen or so species in this subgenus which occur in Europe (mainly in the south) are found in Britain. All the known species are associated with Labiatae.

Key to species

1 Elytra narrower and more parallel-sided, 1·5–1·9 × longer than broad (fig. 149); antennal segments 2–7 and fore tibiae in part obscurely reddish or testaceous (least so in female *cineraceum*) 2

— Elytra broader and more rounded at sides, 1·3–1·5 × longer than broad (fig. 151); antennal segments 2–7 and fore tibiae entirely black (but scape usually reddish). 5

2 Rostrum as long as, or longer than, antennae without club and about as long as head and pronotum combined. . . . . (females) 3

— Rostrum much shorter, shorter than the antennae without club and much shorter than head and pronotum combined. . . . .(males) 4

3 Rostrum longer, longer than head and pronotum together, more shining and strongly curved (fig. 150); fore tibiae at most obscurely reddish or testaceous at base; femora more robust; on *Prunella*. Length 1·7–2·3 mm . . . .**cineraceum** (see below)

— Rostrum shorter, as long as head and pronotum together, duller and much less curved (fig. 153); fore tibiae in greater part reddish or testaceous; femora longer and more slender; predominantly on *Origanum*. Length 1·6–2·0 mm. . . . . **flavimanum** (see below)

4 Rostrum longer, slightly longer than pronotum, more curved and less pubescent, more strongly shining; fore tibiae with a testaceous or reddish ring at base, remainder black; femora more robust (as female). Length 1·7–2·3 mm. . . . . **cineraceum** Wencker
Secondary sexual differences as in key.

On Prunella vulgaris, *especially on the chalk; larval habits unknown, possibly a root-feeder. Local and not generally common but widely distributed in southern England from Dorset eastwards, northwards to Berks, Bucks, and Oxford, with records from W. Gloucester and Chester. Not Wales, Scotland or Ireland. Europe, Caucasus.*

—   Rostrum shorter, shorter than pronotum, straighter and more densely pubescent, dull; fore tibiae ± testaceous or reddish throughout, often obscurely darker at middle; femora more slender and less robust (as female). Length 1·6–2·0 mm . . . . **flavimanum** Gyllenhal
Secondary sexual characters as in key.
On Origanum vulgare, *especially on dry, chalky hillsides, possibly on* Calamintha, Clinopodium *and other species of Labiatae. Larvae in the lower stems. Local. S. Devon, E. and W. Sussex, E. and W. Kent, Surrey, Berks, Bucks and Oxford only. Europe, Anatolia, Caucasus.*

5   Elytra at shoulders much broader than pronotum at base, square, with the humeral prominences strongly evident; basal border of pronotum more strongly dilated (fig. 152); pubescence fine and sparse; size larger, 1·8–2·2 mm; on species of *Mentha*. **vicinum** Kirby
Male with the rostrum shorter, about as long as pronotum, and much shorter than the antennae, duller and less strongly curved. Rostrum of female longer, much longer than pronotum, longer than antennae, more shining and much more strongly curved.
On Mentha *spp., especially* M. aquatica *in fens and damp places. Larvae in stem galls. Rather local but quite widely distributed in England from S. Devon eastwards and northwards to W. Lancaster and Mid W. York. Less common in the Midlands and North and in Wales (Glamorgan). Not Scotland. Irish records require confirmation. Europe eastwards to Siberia, N. Africa.*

—   Elytra rounded at shoulders, little broader than pronotum at base, with the humeral prominences much less evident; basal border of pronotum less strongly dilated (fig. 154); pubescence thicker and denser; size much smaller, 1·1–1·7 mm; on species of *Thymus* . . . .
. . . . **atomarium** Kirby
Male with the rostrum much shorter than the antennae, about as long as pronotum, less strongly curved. Female with rostrum about as long as antennae, much longer than pronotum, more strongly curved.
On Thymus *spp. in dry places. Larvae in stem galls. Common throughout England and Wales as far north as Chester and S.E. York. Not recorded from Scotland or Ireland. Europe eastwards to Mongolia, N. Africa.*

Subgenus **Catapion**

This Palaearctic subgenus, as recognised here, contains some 20 species, of which 3 occur in Britain. Dieckmann (1977) and Hoffmann (1958) are followed in treating *A. curtisii* Stephens (their *A. curtulum* Desbrochers) as a species of *Catapion* rather than *Eutrichapion*, as is done by Kloet & Hincks (1977).

Key to species

1   Head with a depression between eyes and at base of rostrum, so that the eyes project above the top of the head as seen in side view (fig. 155); pronotum strongly transverse; elytra shorter, more rounded at sides, about 1·6 × longer than broad. Length 1·7–2·2 mm . . . . .
. . . . **pubescens** Kirby
Male with the rostrum shorter, much shorter than head and pronotum together, straighter, broader, more pubescent and less shining and with the antennae inserted at middle. Female with the rostrum longer, little shorter than head and pronotum together, narrower, more shining and less pubescent and with the antennae inserted a little behind middle.
Foodplants not known in Britain; on the continent associated with small, yellow-flowered species of Trifolium *(Section* Chronosemian*),* T. campestre, T. aureum *and* T. dubium. *Larvae in stem-galls. Local and not very common, but widely distributed in England and Wales as far north as N.W. and N.E. York and Westmorland. No confirmed records from Scotland and not in Ireland. Europe, Asia to Siberia, N. Africa.*

—   Head between eyes flat or weakly raised, without a depression, eyes in side view not projecting above top of head (figs. 156–159); pronotum quadrate or only slightly transverse; elytra longer, less rounded at sides, about 1·8–2·0 × longer than broad 2

2   Rostrum longer and straighter; in the male about as long as, or little shorter than, and in the female much longer than, the head and pronotum combined (figs. 156, 157). Upper surface

more evidently pubescent, the pubescence obscuring the puncturation of the pronotum; pronotum dull. Length 1·5–2·3 mm................................. **seniculus** Kirby

Male with the antennae inserted just behind middle of rostrum. Female with antennae inserted evidently behind middle. Female with rostrum much longer (as key).

On species of Trifolium. *The biology of the weevil is not well known in Britain but it is probable that the main host is* T. hybridium; *possibly also on* Medicago *spp. Larvae in the stems. Widely distributed and generally common in southern England but becoming rare in the North and Wales, though extending northwards to Edinburgh and the Clyde Isles. Local but widely distributed in Ireland. Europe to Siberia, N. Africa.*

— Rostrum in the male a little longer than the pronotum (fig. 158), in the female evidently shorter than the head and pronotum combined (fig. 159); more strongly curved in both sexes. Upper surface more sparingly pubescent, pubescence not obscuring pronotal puncturation; pronotum somewhat shining. Length 1·6–2·2 mm....... **curtisii** Stephens

Male with the rostrum duller and shorter (as key), with the antennae inserted just behind middle. Female with the rostrum shining, longer and more curved (as key) with the antennae inserted well behind middle, almost at basal third.

Foodplants not well known in Britain, probably Trifolium repens *and* T. fragiferum, *as on the continent. Larvae in galls on the rootstocks. Predominantly, if not exclusively, a maritime species. Local and uncommon. Scattered records in England northwards to E. Suffolk. Inland records, and perhaps those from W. Lancaster and S.E. York, require confirmation. Not recorded from Wales, Scotland or Ireland. Atlantic and Mediterranean coasts of Europe, Asia Minor and N. Africa.*

Subgenus **Diplapion**

This distinctive Palaearctic subgenus contains eight species, of which five occur in Europe; two of these inhabit Britain.

Key to species

1 Furrows between eyes long, twice as long as distance between them, parallel-sided in front, forming a V behind (fig. 162); much less deeply impressed basad; pronotum without or with an indistinct depressed border anteriorly; elytra slightly longer; rostrum distinctly narrowed in front in both sexes; on *Tripleurospermum, Matricaria* and *Anthemis*; [male with penis bluntly rounded at apex]. Length 2·0–2·5 mm.............. **confluens** Kirby

Male with the first segment of the hind tarsus with an inwardly projecting tooth; rostrum shorter than the head and pronotum combined. Female hind tarsus unarmed; rostrum as long as the head and pronotum combined.

In waste places, etc., particularly on the coast, on Tripleurospermum *and* Matricaria *spp. and, less certainly in Britain, on* Anthemis *spp. Larvae in rootstocks, boring downwards from the lower stem. Locally common in England, northwards to W. Norfolk on the east coast but extending much further north on the west coast, to the Isle of Man and Cumberland, and in south-west Scotland from Dumfries to Renfrew. In Wales recorded only from Pembroke. Not in Ireland. Europe, Asia Minor.*

— Furrows between eyes short, shorter than twice the distance between them, forming a U in shape (fig. 163), but more strongly impressed and widened basad; pronotum with a distinct depressed or bevelled border anteriorly; elytra slightly shorter; rostrum less clearly narrowed in front, more nearly parallel-sided; on *Leucanthemum*; [male with penis narrowed and bluntly pointed at apex]. Length 1·8–2·3 mm.......... **stolidum** Germar

Male with the first segment of the hind tarsus toothed, rostrum dilated at insertion of antennae and slightly narrowed in front, shorter than pronotum and head together, less curved. Female with hind tarsus unarmed; rostrum not dilated or narrowed, subcylindrical throughout, as long as, or only a little shorter than, the head and pronotum together, more strongly curved.

On Leucanthemum vulgare. *Biology uncertain, but larvae probably in stems or rootstocks. Local, but widely distributed in southern England, from W. Cornwall to E. Suffolk; rarer further north and in Wales: Hereford, Pembroke, W. Lancaster, Isle of Man. Scottish*

records doubtful. Very local in Ireland: Dublin and Meath only. Europe to mid-Asia, N. Africa.

Subgenus **Taphrotopium**

Two species of this subgenus of seven species occur in western Europe, but only one of them is found in Britain. It is characterised by the very fine, almost obsolete, striae of the elytra, sparsely punctured pronotum, robust and very strongly curved rostrum (figs. 160, 161), the depression between the eyes, and strong humeral prominences.

— Size small, 1.7–2.2 mm . . . . **brunnipes** Boheman

Male smaller, the elytra narrower, subparallel and concolorous with the head and pronotum, black; rostrum shorter, duller and more strongly curved (fig. 160), about as long as, or shorter than, the head and pronotum together and shorter than the antennae. Female larger, the elytra more rounded at sides, broadest at about middle and usually blue, blue-black or purplish; rostrum longer, more shining and less abruptly and strongly curved (fig. 161), longer than, or at least as long as, the head and pronotum together, as long as, or longer than, the antennae.

On species of Filago and Gnaphalium, principally F. vulgaris, in sandy places. The larvae in galls on the flowerheads or leaves of the growing shoots. Very local, in southern England only, and usually rare: N. Devon, W. Kent, Berks, E. and W. Suffolk. Not in Wales, Scotland or Ireland. Central and southern Europe, N. Africa.

Subgenus **Ceratapion**

About 50 species have been described in this predominantly Palaearctic subgenus. Five have been recorded from Britain, but only three are common and the status of the others is dubious. Only four species are recognised in this handbook, but the British representatives of the subgenus need a thorough revision. The colour of the elytra varies from black to blue, blue-black or greenish.

Key to species

1   Rostrum with a tooth on each side at about one-quarter from base, the antennae inserted on the teeth (couplet 14(i) of subgeneric key; fig. 95); pronotum with moderately fine, shallow punctures; striae of elytra moderately fine and shallow; second antennal segment not broader than third; [male with the first segment of the hind tarsi with an inwardly-directed tooth or spur] 2

—   Rostrum slightly dilated at the insertion of the antennae, but not bearing teeth; pronotum with coarse, deep, close, almost rugose, puncturation; striae of elytra broad and deep; second antennal segment broader than third, abruptly dilated from a narrow base (couplet 15(i) of the subgeneric key; fig. 96); [male hind tarsi without a spur or tooth on the first segment]. Length 2·4–2·9 mm . . . . **onopordi** Kirby (fig. 254)

Male with rostrum duller, slightly straighter and shorter, shorter than the head and pronotum together; antennae inserted at about one-third from base; pronotum with sides subparallel, elytra less strongly rounded at sides. Female with the rostrum more shining, more strongly curved and longer, as long as, or longer than, the head and pronotum together; antennae inserted at about one-quarter from base; pronotum more rounded at sides, elytra broader and more rounded at sides.

In grassland, waste places, etc., on a wide variety of Compositae, including species of Arctium, Centaurea and thistles (Carduus, Cirsium, etc.). Larvae in stems. Generally common throughout England and Wales. Very local in Scotland (Dumfries, Lothians, Kintyre and W. Sutherland) but widely distributed. Local and scarce in Ireland (S. Kerry, Dublin). All Europe northwards to Denmark, Caucasus, etc., N. Africa.

2   Larger, broader, more cylindrical and less depressed; elytra strongly rounded at sides, less than twice as long as broad. Length 2·0–3·3 mm; [common, on *Cirsium, Carduus,* etc.].   3

—   Smaller, narrower and more depressed; elytra parallel-sided (in male) or weakly rounded at sides, twice as long as broad (at least in the male). Length 1·6–2·2 mm. [Very rare, on *Centaurea*] . . . .**armatum** Gerstaecker

      Male with the fore tibiae compressed, faceted and shining on the inside, and slightly dilated at apex; first segment of hind tarsi with a strong internal tooth; rostrum shorter and more curved, with the lateral teeth about one-quarter from base. Female with the tibiae and tarsi simple; rostrum longer and less curved, with the lateral teeth at about one-fifth from base.

      In dry places on Centaurea *spp. (in continental Europe). Larvae unknown but probably in stems. Extremely rare in Britain; recorded once from the New Forest (S. Hants). The discoverer, Morley (1941), is vague about numbers taken but an undoubted male is in his collection at the Ipswich Museum. The New Forest locality appears to be atypical for the species, being a damp woodland ride on clay. Europe, as far north as Denmark and southern Sweden.*

3   Proximal segment of hind tarsus with a distinct spine, hook or tooth, directed inwards (figs. 164, 170); fore tibia with an apical or subapical tooth or hook, sometimes only small but usually distinct (figs. 165, 171) . . . .(males) 4

—   Proximal segment of hind tarsus unarmed (figs. 166, 172); fore tibia straight, unarmed, without a trace of a tooth (figs. 167, 173) . . . . (females) 5

4   Tooth of fore tibia small and subapical, occasionally obsolete (fig. 165), tegminal ring of aedeagus slightly shorter and a little more robust (fig. 168), lobes distinctly shorter, with the apices slightly blunter (fig. 169). Eyes larger (fig. 176); rostrum a little longer; puncturation of abdomen slightly stronger and closer; [size larger, 2·8–3·0 mm] (see below). . . . .
. . . .**lacertense** Tottenham

—   Tooth of fore tibia large, strong and pointed, apical (fig. 171); tegminal ring of aedeagus a little longer and less robust (fig. 174), lobes distinctly longer, with the apices slightly more acuminate (fig. 175). Eyes smaller (fig. 179); rostrum a little shorter; puncturation of abdomen a little finer and more remote; [size smaller, 2·0–2·6 mm] (see below) . . . .
. . . . **carduorum** Kirby (fig. 255)

5   Rostral tooth less distinct, blunter and more rounded at sides (fig. 178); rostrum longer, as long as, or only a little shorter than, head and pronotum together (fig. 177). Eyes larger; puncturation of abdomen slightly stronger and closer (as male); [size larger, 3·0–3·3 mm]
. . . .**lacertense** Tottenham

      Sexual differences as in key.

      *On thistles (*Carduus *and* Cirsium *spp., especially* Cirsium vulgare *and* C. arvense. *Biology unknown, but probably a stem-feeder. Not uncommon, but undoubtedly often confused with A. (C.) carduorum. Known from the south of England, from W. Cornwall to S. Essex. Large, brightly-coloured individuals, especially females, from the west and south of Ireland, have been referred to A. (C.) dentirostre Gerstaecker but are not now thought to be that species and are mostly A. lacertense. So far known only from the British Isles; endemic.*

—   Rostral tooth sharper and more pointed, more distinct (fig. 181). Rostrum shorter, distinctly shorter than the head and pronotum together (fig. 180). Eyes smaller; puncturation of abdomen slightly finer and more remote (as male); [size smaller, 2·0–2·9 mm]. . . . .
. . . . **carduorum** Kirby

      Sexual differences as in key.

      On thistles (species of Cirsium *and* Carduus). *Larvae in the stems. Common and generally abundant throughout the British Isles. More local in Scotland than in England and Wales, but extending to Caithness, though not reported from the Outer Hebrides, Orkney or Zetland. Widely distributed in Ireland. All Europe and probably throughout the Palaearctic.*

Subgenus **Omphalapion**

Eight species of this subgenus, all with the characteristic globular pronotum, are found in the Palaearctic region, of which five inhabit western Europe and three the British Isles.

Key to species

1   Pronotum with a shallow, fine, narrow, somewhat obsolete longitudinal line or impression at base, or with the line evanescent or wanting (figs. 183, 186); pronotum finely but closely punctured, dull. [Female with rostrum shorter, not longer than head and pronotum together (fig. 182)]. On average smaller, 1·6–2·4 mm 2

—   Pronotum with a strong, deep and wide fovea, furrow or longitudinal impression, always clearly evident and never evanescent or wanting (fig. 185); pronotum coarsely and closely punctured, interspaces shining. [Female with rostrum very long, much longer than the head and pronotum together (fig. 184)]. Generally larger, 1·8–2·8 mm . . **sorbi** (Fabricius)

Male smaller, 1·8–2·4 mm, with elytra black; rostrum more strongly curved and robust, short, as long as head and pronotum combined, or much shorter. Female larger, 2·2–2·8 mm, with the elytra blue; rostrum much straighter, proportionally more slender and longer, evidently longer than the head and pronotum combined (fig. 184).

On species of Anthemis *and* Matricaria *(on the continent, foodplants not recorded in Britain). Larvae in the capitula. Rare, or rather extremely local in Britain, but often abundant when found. Scattered records, but widely distributed, in England, Wales and Scotland from N. Devon and W. Kent to Kirkcudbright and Edinburgh. Absent from Ireland. Europe, Anatolia and the Caucasus.*

2   Rostrum slightly constricted at base and so with a weak dilation at insertion of the antennae; elytra shorter and proportionally more rounded at sides, about 1·3 × longer than broad: pronotum moderately and uniformly rounded at sides (fig. 186), not angled, more finely and less closely punctured; size smaller, 1·5–2·6 mm. . . . .**dispar** Germar

Male smaller, 1·5–2·1 mm; entirely black; rostrum about as long as, or a little longer than, the pronotum. Female larger, 1·7–2·6 mm; black, with a bluish or greenish sheen on the elytra; rostrum as long as, or longer than, the head and pronotum combined.

In grassy places, on the continent on species of Anthemis *and only exceptionally on* Matricaria *(? and* Tripleurospermum*) spp., but foodplants in Britain not recorded. Biology imperfectly known, but larvae probably in capitula. Rare and discovered only recently (Dolling 1975); known from a few localities in E. Kent. Europe, Asia Minor, and N. Africa, but status and taxonomy long confused (Dieckmann 1977) and distribution therefore uncertain.*

—   Rostrum not constricted at base and so not, or scarcely, dilated at insertion of the antennae; elytra longer and proportionally less rounded at sides, about 1·4 × longer than broad; pronotum more strongly rounded at sides, often angled in middle and more or less hexagonal (fig. 183); more strongly and closely punctured; size larger, 1·6–2·8 mm . . . . **hookeri** Kirby

Male unicolorous black; with rostrum short, duller, more robust, shorter than the pronotum, antennae inserted at about one-third from base; size on average smaller, 1·6–2·0 mm. Female with the elytra blue, blue-green or black with a violet tinge; rostrum longer, more shining and slender, as long as, or longer than, the pronotum, antennae inserted at about one-quarter from base; size larger, 1·9–2·8 mm.

In waste places, etc., on Tripleurospermum spp. *and possibly also on species of* Matricaria. *Larvae in the capitula. Widely distributed throughout England and Wales to Chester and N. E. and Mid.-W. York. Generally common in the south of England, but becoming rarer further north. Not recorded from Scotland or Ireland. Europe, N. Africa and Asia Minor.*

Subgenus **Synapion**

This group is characterised by the very small scutellum, which occasionally cannot be seen at all, the absence of shoulders, and the sinuate side margins of the pronotum (figs 82, 83). About ten species are known from the Palaearctic, but only one occurs in the British Isles. The elytral striae are broad but shallow, the elytra ovoid and the pronotum very finely and diffusely punctured; the colour is entirely unicolorous black.

—   Length 2·2–2·8 mm. . . . . **ebeninum** Kirby (fig. 76)

49

Male with the rostrum more robust, only about as long as the pronotum. Female with the rostrum more slender, as long as, or scarcely shorter than, the head and pronotum together. Other sexual differences very slight.

On a variety of Papilionaceae abroad but in Britain predominantly on Lotus uliginosus and thus in damp places. Larvae in the stems. Widespread but rather local in England and Wales, less common in the north, and just extending into southern Scotland: Dumfries only. Not in Ireland. All Europe, Caucasus.

Subgenus **Pirapion**

Four species of this subgenus are known in the Palaearctic region and two of these are found in Britain. *Pirapion* is immediately characterised by the shape of the elytra, which are broader behind the middle, greatly dilated posteriad (visible both from above and in profile), and with very weak shoulders (figs. 189, 190, 193, 194). Both our species feed on Papilionaceae-Genistae, particularly *Cytisus scoparius*. *A. (P.) atratulum* Germar is much more familiar to British coleopterists as *A. (P.) striatum* Kirby.

Key to species

1 Head distinctly striated between eyes and coarsely punctured behind to junction with prono-
tum (fig. 188); pronotum with a longitudinal depression at base only, not extending to middle, and often obscure or wanting altogether (fig. 188); generally smaller, 2·0–2·8 mm, and with the elytra less dilated behind (figs. 189, 190), ratio of length/breadth ranging from 1·26–1·35. [Male with the first tarsal segment of all legs with a distinct curved tooth or hook, projecting inwards and downwards (fig. 187)] .... **immune** Kirby
Male with the rostrum a little shorter, not as long as the head and pronotum together, broader and straighter; first tarsal segment distinctly toothed (fig. 187); elytra often slightly less dilated (fig. 189). Rostrum of female longer, as long as head and pronotum combined, more slender and less curved; tarsal segments unarmed; elytra often more strongly dilated (fig. 190).

Probably exclusively on Cytisus scoparius *in Britain and hence mainly on heaths and sandy areas. Possibly also on* Genista spp., *but no breeding records. Larvae in galls on young stems. Rather local, but widely distributed throughout Great Britain as far north as Elgin; few records from Wales and Midland England. Scarce and very local in Ireland: Wexford, Meath and Armagh only. Europe as far north as Denmark and eastwards to the Caucasus; Algeria.*

— Head finely punctured or obscurely alutaceous between eyes, not striated; base of head not punctured, shining and with very fine transverse lines (fig. 192); pronotum with a distinct, fine, longitudinal depression which runs for almost all of its length and always beyond the middle but which is evanescent at extreme base and apex (fig. 192); usually larger, 2·2–3·1 mm, and with the elytra more strongly dilated behind (figs. 193, 194), ratio of length/breadth ranging from 1·12–1·25; [tarsi of both sexes unarmed (male, fig. 191)] ....
.... **atratulum** Germar (fig. 256)
Sexes very similar; male with the rostrum slightly shorter, as long as the head and pronotum combined. Female with the rostrum a little longer than the head and pronotum combined.

Predominantly on Cytisus scoparius, *also occasionally on other papilionaceous shrubs (Genista) such as* Ulex europaeus *and* Genista spp. *Larvae in galls in young stems. Generally common throughout England and Wales. More local and less common in Scotland, but extending northwards to E. Ross; not recorded from the Ebudes or Outer Hebrides. Widely distributed in Ireland. Europe; Algeria.*

Subgenus **Melanapion**

This subgenus, which contains only two species, was included in *Eutrichapion* by Hoffmann (1958), Kloet & Hincks (1977) and also, with some reservations, by

Kissinger (1968), but its affinities may lie closer to the *Taeniapion-Thymapion* group of subgenera. One species is known in Britain; it is characterised by the very narrow, carinate interstices of the elytra and the broad, deep striae (fig. 106).

—   Colour entirely black, length 1·7–2·2 mm. . . . . **minimum** Herbst

Male with the rostrum shorter, as long as pronotum; form shorter and stouter, the elytra about 1·38× longer than broad. Female with the rostrum longer, evidently longer than the pronotum; form more elongate, the elytra about 1·48× longer than broad.

On a wide variety of Salix *spp., both broad- and narrow-leaved species. The larvae are inquilines in the galls of* Pontania *spp. (Hym., Tenthredinidae) and, according to Hoffmann (1958), in those of Cecidomyidae (Dipt.) as well. Very local in the British Isles and generally rare, but widely distributed through England and Wales as far north as Chester and also recorded from Kirkcudbright and, more doubtfully, from Dumfries. Not in Ireland. Europe and Asia to Mongolia.*

Subgenus **Trichapion**

Although included by both Hoffmann (1958) and Kloet & Hincks (1977) in the subgenus *Eutrichapion, Trichapion* is a very distinct subgenus which is very poorly represented in the Palaearctic but rich in species in both South and North America, where well over 100 species are known (Kissinger 1968). All *Trichapion* species have the mesothoracic tibiae armed with an apical tooth, hook or mucro in the male (fig. 195); only some species (none British) of *Eutrichapion* have such a structure. Only one species of *Trichapion* is known from Europe, including Britain.

—   Small (1·8–2·4 mm), entirely black, often with a slight brassy sheen, and with a conspicuous fringe of white setae just under the eye (fig. 197); the thoracic epimera are also clothed with white setae. Pronotum bordered at base . . . . **simile** Kirby

Male with the middle and hind tibiae armed with a tooth apically (fig. 195); rostrum short, little longer than the pronotum. Female with all the tibiae unarmed (fig. 196); rostrum considerably longer, usually much longer, but occasionally only a little longer, than the head and pronotum together.

In woods, heaths, etc., on species of Betula. *Larvae in the female catkins. Somewhat local, but often abundant where it occurs, and widely distributed throughout England. Apparently rarer in Wales (Merioneth only) and Scotland (Kirkcudbright, Mid Perth and Elgin), and not recorded from Ireland. Holarctic (Europe, Algeria, Asia Minor, Siberia, Canada, USA).*

Subgenus **Pseudotrichapion**

Until a late stage in the preparation of this handbook, it was intended to use the name *Apion s. str.* for this group, following Hoffmann (1958). The (correct) use of *Apion s. str.* for the group previously known as *Erythrapion* Schilsky has left the subgenus under consideration without a name. From the subgeneric names which appear to be available, *Pseudotrichapion* has been chosen on purely pragmatic grounds as the most convenient and practical name. Dieckmann (1977) used it for three continental species, including *A. punctigerum,* but Hoffmann (1958) stated that *A. aethiops* (and another species) formed part of the subgenus. A comprehensive taxonomic review of the group, and the related subgenus *Eutrichapion,* in which Kissinger (1968) included the four species currently included in *Pseudotrichapion,* is needed. These species can be distinguished from those of *Eutrichapion* by the glabrous upper surface. As recognised here, *Pseudotrichapion* contains about 22 species in the Palaearctic region.

Key to species

1   Elytra bright blue or blue-black; [pronotum black, or concolorous with elytra]; pronotal depression distinct only at base and usually obscure, not forming a distinct longitudinal furrow and rarely extending as far as the middle of the pronotum (fig. 201); elytra broad, 1·20–1·39 × longer than broad (sometimes a little longer in *A. (A.) aethiops*) 2

—   Whole upper surface bright golden-green, green or blue-green; pronotum with a distinct longitudinal furrow, extending from near base at least to middle of pronotum (fig. 200); elytra less broad, 1·40–1·50 × longer than broad .... **astragali** (Paykull)
     Male with the rostrum shorter, shorter than the head and pronotum combined and also shorter than fore tibia. Female with rostrum longer, nearly as long as the head and pronotum combined and distinctly longer than fore tibia.
     Exclusively on Astragalus glycyphyllos *in Britain. Larvae in flower buds. Very local, though often abundant where it occurs, in England from N. Somerset to E. Sussex and northwards to N. Lincoln; records from further north need confirmation. Not recorded from Wales or Ireland and very doubtfully from Scotland. Europe, Asia to Mongolia, N. Africa.*

2   Pronotum coarsely or moderately punctured, alutaceous but shining between punctures, sides simply rounded or very weakly sinuate (fig. 201, 203), usually black, not concolorous with elytra; head narrower, width across eyes distinctly less than at base, punctured or obscurely striated between eyes; elytral striae deep and broad, half as broad as interstices; less robust and smaller species, 1·9–2·9 mm 3

—   Pronotum finely and diffusely punctured, strongly alutaceous and dull between punctures, sides sinuate and more strongly rounded (fig. 198), steely blue, concolorous with elytra; head broader, width across eyes equal to width at base, or nearly so, distinctly striated between eyes; elytral striae shallow and narrower, much less than half as broad as interstices; a larger and more robust species, 2·2–3·2 mm .... **punctigerum** (Paykull)
     Male with rostrum alutaceous and dull to apex, of almost equal width throughout, antennae inserted at middle or slightly in front of middle. Female with the apical half of the rostrum shining and distinctly narrowed distad, antennae inserted behind middle (fig. 199).
     In waste places, wood edges, roadsides, etc. on species of Vicia, *particularly* V. sepium. *Larvae in the pods. Rather local, but widely distributed throughout England and Wales from W. Cornwall and E. Kent to Cumberland and the Isle of Man. Very local in Scotland: Kirkcudbright, Edinburgh, Kincardine and Orkney only. Not recorded from Ireland. Europe, Asia Minor, N. Africa.*

3   Pronotum strongly transverse (fig. 201), coarsely and deeply punctured; head broad, strongly punctured behind eyes, which are protuberant (fig. 202); elytra broader, 1·21–1·27 × longer than broad; antennal club broad, about twice as long as broad. [Length 2·2–2·9 mm] .... **pisi** (Fabricius)
     Male with the rostrum short and straighter, shorter than the head and pronotum combined and with the antennae inserted nearer to apex, at nearly two-thirds from base. Female with the rostrum long and more curved, longer than the head and pronotum together, and with the antennae inserted nearer the base, only just in front of middle.
     Biology in Britain not well known. Probably exclusively on Medicago spp., *as in continental Europe (Dieckmann 1977); on* M. falcata *and* M. lupulina *and a pest of* M. sativa. *The larvae develop in late autumn in vegetative buds and pupate and then emerge as adults in spring. Generally common throughout England; Isle of Man. Few Welsh records. One small area of distribution around Firth of Forth in Scotland (Berwick, Haddington, Edinburgh and Fife only). Quite widely distributed but not common in Ireland. Throughout the Palaearctic region.*

—   Pronotum less strongly transverse to quadrate (fig. 203), moderately but rather shallowly punctured; head narrow, finely and obscurely punctured or unpunctured behind eyes, which are not protuberant but almost flat (fig. 203); elytra narrower, usually 1·31–1·39 × longer than broad, but occasionally even narrower; antennal club narrow, about 3 × longer than broad; (length 1·9–2·7 mm) .... **aethiops** Herbst
     Male with the rostrum shorter than the head and pronotum combined (but males apparently very much less common than females in the British Isles). Female with the rostrum as long as head and pronotum combined.
     On roadsides, waste places and in lightly-wooded areas, on species of Vicia, *particularly* V. cracca *and* V. sepium. *Larvae in stem galls. Widely distributed and usually common throughout England, including the Isle of Man. Wales: Glamorgan and Carmarthen. Widely*

distributed in mainland Scotland from the Borders to W. Sutherland and Caithness but not recorded from the Ebudes or Outer Hebrides, nor from Orkney or Zetland. Widespread in Ireland. Throughout the Palaearctic region.

Subgenus **Eutrichapion**

Although the 15 species assigned to this subgenus here are somewhat different in general facies, all have the characteristic pubescence and absence of midtibial hooks in the male, which are characteristic but not diagnostic of the subgenus. It is likely that further work will result in its division into several subgenera. There are more than 30 species known from the Palaearctic and the group is also represented in the Nearctic region.

Key to species

1   Legs entirely dark, usually black 2
—   Legs in large part yellow, reddish-yellow or red, at least femora (except apices) and pro-thoracic tibiae; [pronotum transverse; antennae with at least base yellow; elytra short-oval; size rather small, length 1·9–2·4 mm] . . . . **viciae** (Paykull)
    Male with the apices of the femora more narrowly darkened; middle tibiae and fore tarsi more generally yellow or red and with a testaceous ring near base of the hind tibiae; antennae, including club, entirely yellow or red; rostrum shorter, about as long as the pronotum, more pubescent at base, antennae inserted slightly behind middle; elytra narrower. Female with the femora more broadly darkened apically; middle tibiae, fore tarsi and hind tibiae more generally darkened, the first with an obscure and narrow testaceous ring proximad; antennae with base yellow, club and distal segments of funiculus black; rostrum longer, evidently longer than the pronotum, less pubescent at base, antennae inserted more evidently behind middle; elytra broader.
    In hedgerows, roadsides, etc., on species of Vicia, *particularly* V. cracca, *and* Lathyrus pratensis. *In continental Europe the larvae feed on the anthers and pistils of the flowers, not in pods. Widespread and usually abundant throughout England (including Isle of Man) but recorded from only Glamorgan and Pembroke in Wales. Widely distributed in Scotland to W. Sutherland and Caithness, but not recorded from the Outer Hebrides, Orkney or Zetland. Widespread, but generally much less common, in Ireland. Palaearctic region.*
2   Pronotum with a median longitudinal channel extending from base to beyond middle (best seen in lateral view) (e.g. fig. 204) 3
—   Pronotum with median longitudinal channel distinct only at base, not extending beyond middle, and often faint or obscure 6
3   Head without a depression between eyes; pronotum not, or scarcely, transverse; elytra black, or if blue then head across eyes very narrow 4
—   Head with a distinct depression between eyes (figs 204, 205); pronotum strongly transverse and much narrower at apex than at base (fig. 204); elytra blue; [pubescence sparse; length 1·9–2·5 mm] . . . . **spencii** Kirby
    Male with the eyes larger and more protuberant, head distinctly broadest across eyes (fig. 204); rostrum parallel-sided beyond antennal insertion and pubescent to apex. Female with the eyes smaller and less protuberant, head distinctly broadest at base (fig. 205); rostrum slightly narrowed proximad of antennal insertion and much less pubescent.
    Generally in damp places, particularly in fens, but also on roadsides, etc., on species of Vicia, *especially* V. cracca. *Biology unknown. Somewhat local, but widely distributed throughout mainland England from Dorset and N. Somerset eastwards, and often common. Widely distributed in Scotland to W. Sutherland, Caithness and Orkney, but not recorded from the Outer Hebrides or Zetland, nor many other Scottish vice-counties. Absent from the Isle of Man and Ireland. Europe, central Siberia and N. Africa.*
4   Antennae entirely black, or with at most extreme base of scape yellowish to pitchy; eyes less protuberant, head broadest at base 5
—   Antennae with at least the first three segments yellow or yellowish-red; segments 4 and 5 pitchy or yellow to red; eyes more protuberant, head broadest across eyes; [pronotal furrow rarely complete, evanescent distad (fig. 206); length 2·0–2·4 mm] . . . . . . **ervi** Kirby

Male with the antennae (including club) entirely yellow, yellowish-red or pitchy; rostrum shorter than pronotum, pubescent, antennae inserted at about middle. Female with antennal club and distal segments black (at least basal three segments yellow), middle segments pitchy; rostrum longer than pronotum, glabrous except at extreme base, antennae inserted well behind middle.

In waste places, etc., and particularly in hedgerows. Most frequently on Lathyrus pratensis; *also on species of* Vicia. *Larvae in flower buds. Widespread and abundant throughout the British Isles, though less common in northern Scotland (to E. Ross and Orkney) and not recorded from the Outer Hebrides or Zetland; common in Ireland. All the Palaearctic region.*

5   Pronotal furrow seldom complete to apex; scape less abruptly dilated at apex, first funicular segment more elongate and less globose; rostrum in both sexes longer than head and pronotum combined; upper surface very sparsely pubescent 6

—   Pronotal furrow usually distinct to apex or evanescent only very close to apical margin; scape abruptly dilated at apex, first funicular segment broader and more globose in comparison with the second (fig. 211); rostrum in both sexes shorter than head and pronotum together; upper surface much more distinctly pubescent . . . . **ononis** Kirby

Male with the rostrum shorter and more pubescent, scarcely longer than the pronotum; elytra narrower and more parallel-sided. Female with the rostrum distinctly longer than the pronotum and little shorter than the head and pronotum together, less pubescent; elytra broader and more rounded at sides.

Generally in dry places, on Ononis repens *and* O. spinosa. *Larvae in the pods, feeding on the unripe seeds. Widespread and locally abundant in England and Wales; less common in Scotland, but extending as far north as Elgin. Not recorded from Isle of Man or Ireland; there is no basis for the statement in Fowler (1891) that 'in Ireland it is most likely general'. Europe, Asia Minor, N. Africa.*

6   Legs shorter, middle legs little longer, often shorter, than elytra; first segment of fore tarsus shorter than remainder (without claws); antennae entirely black, or at most with scape obscurely testaceous at base; rostrum strongly curved in both sexes 7

—   Legs longer, middle legs evidently longer than elytra; first segment of fore tarsus long and slender, as long as, or longer than, remainder of tarsus (without claws) (figs. 207, 208); antennae with scape and first funicular segment clear yellow, funicular segments 2 and 3 yellow to testaceous or pitchy; rostrum nearly straight in female, only slightly curved in male; [eyes large but not protuberant; elytra blue, large species, 2·3–2·9 mm] . . . .
. . . . **vorax** Herbst

Male with the fore tibiae 'twisted', flattened, broadened and sinuate on the inner side (fig. 207); first tarsal segment, especially the metathoracic, longer and narrower (fig. 209); second funicular segment clear yellow; rostrum shorter than head and pronotum combined, pubescent nearly to apex, slightly dilated at antennal insertion and curved or bent distally from this point; antennae inserted in front of middle. Female with the fore tibiae simple (fig. 208); first tarsal segment shorter and broader (fig. 210); second funicular segment pitchy or testaceous; rostrum longer than the head and pronotum combined, less pubescent, and almost glabrous from antennal insertion to apex, not dilated at antennal insertion, very slightly curved, almost straight; antennae inserted behind middle.

In hedgerows and waste places and often in woods on trees, shrubs and ground vegetation. The hosts are Vicia *spp., and the weevil is unusual in being a vector of plant viruses which attack beans, etc. (Cockbain et al. 1982). Larvae in the flowers. Widespread and generally common in England but recorded only from Glamorgan in Wales. In Scotland to Renfrew and the Lothians. Widely distributed but less common in Ireland. Europe, Siberia, Asia Minor, N. Africa.*

7   Pronotum transverse to quadrate, conical or strongly rounded at sides; elytra short-oval, or if elongate, not depressed on disc. [Generally larger and more robust species, 1·9–3·3 mm]
. . . . 9

—   Pronotum quadrate, or nearly so, to distinctly elongate, cylindrical, sides subparallel (figs. 212, 216); elytra elongate, long-oval, broadest behind middle and depressed on disc; [head long, sides subparallel] 8

8   Size larger, 2·1–2·7 mm. Head with a distinct glabrous, shining, transverse band at base, transversely striate, but unpunctured, distinctly demarcated from the strongly punctured remainder of the head (width of glabrous band about equal to, or a little less than, the punctured area behind the eyes) (fig. 217); pronotum more strongly and closely punctured, interspaces narrower than punctures (fig. 212); rostrum longer (compare same sex);

[aedeagus relatively much larger, about 0·3 × body length, apex truncate (fig. 214), sharply angled in profile (fig. 215); on *Onobrychis*] . . . . **intermedium** Eppelsheim

Male with the rostrum less strongly curved, nearly twice as long as the head, but distinctly shorter than the head and pronotum together, pubescent nearly to apex; antennae inserted only a little behind middle. Female with the rostrum more strongly curved, longer, about as long as the head and pronotum combined and more than twice as long as the head alone, glabrous or sparsely pubescent at base only; antennae inserted at about two-fifths from base, conspicuously behind middle.

On calcareous grasslands and cliffs. On Onobrychis viciifolia, *larvae in the stems. A recent discovery in Britain (Parry 1982) and known so far from only E. Kent and E. and W. Sussex. Southern and mid-Europe to W. Siberia.*

— Size smaller, 1·6–2·3 mm. Head without a basal glabrous band, punctured or shagreened to junction with pronotum (fig. 213); pronotum with puncturation shallower and more remote, interspaces as broad as, or broader than, punctures (fig. 216); rostrum shorter (in each corresponding sex); [aedeagus relatively much smaller, about 0·2 × body length, apex rounded (fig. 218), not sharply angled in profile (fig. 219); on *Medicago*] . . . . **tenue** Kirby

Male with the rostrum shorter and straighter, little longer than pronotum, and sparsely pubescent nearly to apex. Female with the rostrum longer and more curved, much longer than the pronotum and little shorter than the head and pronotum together, glabrous, though dull distally from antennal insertion; [antennae inserted at about middle in both sexes].

In grasslands, etc., on species of Medicago, *particularly* M. lupulina, *and possibly on other Papilionaceae, but hosts not well known in Britain. Larvae in stems. Widely distributed and often common in southern England, but becoming less common northwards and in Wales. Recorded from only Dumfries, Haddington and Edinburgh in Scotland, and not known from Ireland. Probably throughout the Palearctic.*

9 Elytra blue, short-oval, not more than 1·39 × longer than broad (figs. 220, 221, 223, 224), moderately to densely pubescent. [Eyes neither protuberant nor flattened, width of head across eyes about equal to width at base; upper surface of head and pronotum dull, closely and distinctly punctured and without a brassy or greenish reflection] 10

— Elytra black, long-oval, at least 1·40 × longer than broad, or if blue then much more elongate, up to 1·72 × longer than broad (figs. 229, 231), and much less densely pubescent 11

10 Very distinctly pubescent; pronotum more finely, shallowly and closely punctured, duller, the interspaces more strongly shagreened (fig. 225); colour of elytra generally less bright blue; median basal depression of pronotum short, narrow, finer and shallower and of a more nearly even width throughout except basad (fig. 225); size smaller, 1·9–2·3 mm . . . . **waltoni** Stephens

Male with the rostrum about as long as the pronotum, more distinctly pubescent, almost to apex; antennae inserted at, or just in front of, middle. Female with rostrum much longer than pronotum, nearly as long as the head and pronotum combined, less pubescent and with the apical part glabrous; antennae inserted behind middle.

In calcareous grasslands, mainly, if not exclusively, on the chalk and oolitic limestone (restricted by the occurrence of its foodplant). On Hippocrepis comosa *and probably exclusively so in Britain. Larvae semi-exposed in stems (Morris 1983). Local, but not uncommon, in the chalk and limestone counties of southern England from Dorset and N. and S. Wilts. to E. Kent and northwards to E. Gloucester, Bucks, Oxford and Bedford. More isolated records from E. Cornwall, Leicester and W. Lancaster need confirmation. Not recorded from Wales, Scotland or Ireland. Not widely distributed in Europe: France, Germany (DDR), Switzerland, Italy and Spain.*

— Less distinctly pubescent; pronotum more coarsely and deeply and less closely punctured, more shining, the interspaces less strongly shagreened (fig. 222); colour of elytra generally brighter blue; median basal depression of pronotum longer, usually distinct to middle, broader, deeper and expanded towards base (fig. 222); size larger, 2·1–2·8 mm . . . . **reflexum** Gyllenhal

Male with the rostrum shorter than the head and pronotum together, pubescent to apex, relatively more robust and parallel-sided; antennae inserted in front of middle. Female with the rostrum much longer, nearly half as long again as head and pronotum together, less pubescent and somewhat narrowed sub-distally; antennae inserted at the mid-point.

Mainly in calcareous grasslands, exclusively on Onobrychis viciifolia. *Larvae perhaps in galls in the inforescences, but biology not well known. Particularly in the chalk counties of*

55

England, from N. and S. Somerset eastwards to E. Kent and northwards to Hereford, Warwick and Cambridge, with more isolated records from N.E. York and, more doubtfully, S. Lancaster. Not recorded from Wales, Scotland or Ireland. Europe (except Scandinavia), Siberia, Asia, N. Africa.

11   Pronotum closely, coarsely and more deeply punctured; head finely striated between eyes, dull; eyes not protruberant; head and pronotum black, without any brassy or greenish reflection; upper surface sparsely but distinctly pubescent 12

—   Pronotum diffusely, finely and more shallowly punctured (fig. 226); head not striated between eyes, alutaceous and rather shining; eyes protruberant (fig. 226); head and pronotum often with a brassy or greenish reflection; upper surface very sparsely and less distinctly pubescent; [elytra blue or greenish; striae deep; size small, 1·8–2·6 mm . . . .
. . . . **virens** Herbst

Male with the rostrum much straighter and shorter, as long as, or shorter than, the pronotum (fig. 227); sparsely pubescent to apex and duller; antennae inserted at, or a little in front of, middle. Female with the rostrum much more strongly curved and longer, considerably longer than the pronotum and little shorter than the head and pronotum together (fig. 228); sparsely pubescent but strongly shining; antennae inserted a little behind middle.

In a wide variety of open and grassy biotopes, including sand dunes and agricultural land. On species of Trifolium, *particularly T.* repens *but possibly also T.* pratense *and other species; not apparently on other Papilionaceae. Larvae in stems. Widespread and generally abundant throughout England and Wales. More local in Scotland, to W. Sutherland but few records north of Fife and not recorded from the Outer Hebrides, Orkney or Zetland (though widespread in the Ebudes). Widespread and often common in Ireland. Throughout the Palaearctic region.*

12   Elytra more elongate, generally at least 1·70 × longer than broad (1·62–1·76); evenly rounded at sides and broadest at about middle, shoulders not marked (figs. 229, 231); pronotum elongate, evenly rounded at sides and not markedly conical 13

—   Elytra less elongate, usually not more than 1·60 × longer than broad (1·40–1·62) and more abruptly contracted to apex so less evenly rounded at sides, often broadest behind middle, and with shoulders more evident (figs. 234, 236, 237, 240, 242, 244); pronotum quadrate or slightly transverse, more markedly conical, narrower at apex than at base. 14

13   Scutellum large and deeply-seated and with a median, longitudinal furrow; elytra shorter (fig. 229), more pubescent and dull, with strong microsculpture of transverse striations; rostrum more strongly curved (especially in the female) (fig. 230); eyes larger and flatter, head distinctly broader at base than across eyes; head shorter, about as broad as long; pronotum more strongly and deeply punctured and more pubescent; [on *Ulex*; length 2·5–3·3 mm]. . . . . **scutellare** Kirby

Male with the rostrum straighter, more parallel-sided and shorter, about as long as, or a little longer than, the head and pronotum together; antennae inserted nearer middle, at about two-fifths from base. Female with the rostrum much more strongly curved (fig. 230), apical half with sides concave, and longer, at least one-quarter longer than head and pronotum together; antennae inserted nearer base at nearly two-thirds from apex.

On heaths; particularly on Ulex minor, *also on U.* europaeus *(though by no means general on that species) and possibly U.* gallii. *Larvae in conspicuous stem-galls. Widespread in England and Wales, but with a patchy distribution and distinctly less common in the north, though recorded from Scotland (Kirkcudbright only). Local though fairly widespread in southern Ireland to Wicklow and Dublin and with a more isolated record from W. Mayo. Isle of Man. An Atlantic distribution: France, northern Spain and Portugal. Absent from central, southern and eastern Europe.*

—   Scutellum small, simple; elytra long (fig. 231), less pubescent and more shining with the cross striations of the microsculpture less strong and distinct; rostrum straighter, not so strongly curved in either sex (fig. 232); eyes smaller and more outstanding, head almost as broad across eyes as at base; head longer, distinctly longer than broad; pronotum finely and more shallowly punctured, more finely and less distinctly pubescent; [on *Melilotus*; length 2·2–3·3 mm . . . . **meliloti** Kirby

Male with the rostrum shorter, slightly straighter, more robust and slightly more pubescent, clearly shorter than the head and pronotum combined. Female with the rostrum longer, a little more curved (fig. 232), less robust and slightly less pubescent, about as long as the head and pronotum combined, or a little less.

56

In waste places, roadsides, etc. On species of Melilotus, *particularly* M. officinalis *but also on* M. alba *and probably other species. Larvae in stems. Widely distributed and locally common in southern England from N. Somerset eastwards as far north as Mid W. Yorks. Few records from Wales and none from Scotland or Ireland. Europe, Asia, N. Africa.*

14 Tarsi with the first segment longer, at least twice as long as broad (figs. 233, 235); antennae longer and more slender, segment 3 about 2 × longer than broad, scape nearly as long as club; pronotum coarsely punctured; shoulders prominent and well-marked; [on *Vicia* and *Lathyrus* spp.] 15

— Tarsi with the first segment shorter, about $1\frac{1}{3}$ × longer than broad on the fore and middle legs (figs. 238, 243) and a little less than 2 × on the hind legs; antennae shorter and more robust, segment 2 not more than $1\frac{1}{2}$ × longer than broad, scape distinctly shorter than club; pronotum moderately punctured; shoulders less prominent; [on *Lotus* spp.] 16

15 Eyes almost flat (figs. 249, 250), much less prominent, longitudinally elongate (fig. 251); head longer than broad (figs. 249, 250); pronotum smaller in relation to elytra, more strongly conical, width at base greater than that at apex. Length 2·3–2·9 mm. . . . **gyllenhali** Kirby
Male with the eyes less flat, head narrower basad (fig. 249); sides subparallel; rostrum more pubescent and robust, a little shorter than the head and pronotum combined; antennae inserted just in front of middle; elytra narrower, about 1·57 × longer than broad. Female with the eyes flatter, head broader basad (fig. 250); sides divergent to base; rostrum less pubescent and more slender, longer than the head and pronotum combined; antennae inserted at middle of rostrum; elytra broader, about 1·43 × longer than broad.
In hedgerows, waysides and at wood edges. On a variety of Vicia *spp., but probably chiefly on* V. cracca *in Britain. Larvae in stem galls. Widely distributed, but local, throughout England and Wales and not recorded from several vice-counties, particularly in the south Midlands. In Scotland as far north as Ayr and Fife. Widely distributed in Ireland, but perhaps less common than the literature suggests. Europe eastwards to mid-Siberia.*

— Eyes not flat, more prominent, round (fig. 248); head broader than long (fig. 247); pronotum larger in relation to elytra, much less conical, width at base only slightly greater than at apex. Length 2·0–2·5 mm . . . . **afer** Gyllenhal
Male with the rostrum more robust, narrowed at apex, and shorter, not as long as the head and pronotum together; antennae inserted at, or a little behind, middle; eyes more prominent. Female with the rostrum more slender, parallel-sided throughout its length, and longer, considerably longer than head and pronotum together; antennae inserted behind middle; eyes a little smaller and less prominent.
In hedgerows, wood edges and waysides. Following Dieckmann's clarification (1976, 1977) of the status of A. afer *and* A. platalea, *known to be probably exclusively on* Lathyrus pratensis *and not on species of* Vicia *on the continent (cf. Fowler 1891), but foodplants requiring investigation in Britain. Larvae in vegetative buds. Local, but widely distributed throughout England from S. Somerset eastwards and northwards to Northumberland South and Cumberland. Few records from Wales (Glamorgan, Brecon and Denbigh) and recorded only from Dumfries in Scotland. No Irish records. Europe, except the north, eastwards to W. Siberia.*

16 Elytra more sharply rounded at sides, more strongly broadened behind (especially in the male), and broadest behind middle (figs. 242, 244); dorsum more strongly shining, elytra with a weak metallic reflection, dark blue to dark bronze-green; rostrum usually a little more slender; [apex of penis rounded (fig. 245); on *Lotus uliginosus*]. Length 2·0–2·5 mm. . . . . **modestum** Germar
Male with the rostrum as long as the head and pronotum together; elytra broader behind middle and less rounded at sides (fig. 244). Female with the rostrum a little longer than the head and pronotum together; elytra less broad behind middle, more rounded at sides (fig. 242).
In marshes, wet meadows and other damp places, on Lotus uliginosus *(and not on other species of* Lotus*). Larvae in the pods. Only recently discovered in Britain (Dieckmann 1973, Morris 1976a), and so far recorded from only Dorset, S. Hants, W. Kent, Shropshire, Glamorgan and Pembroke, but likely to be much more widespread. Europe as far north as Sweden, N. Africa.*

— Elytra more smoothly rounded at sides, less strongly broadened behind, and broadest at about middle (figs. 237, 240); dorsum duller, less shining, elytra without a weak metallic reflection, black; rostrum slightly more robust; [apex of penis acuminate (fig. 241); principally on *Lotus corniculatus*]. Length 2·0–2·5 mm . . . . **loti** Kirby (fig. 319)

Male with the rostrum generally shorter, a little shorter than the head and pronotum together. Female with the rostrum usually longer, about as long as head and pronotum together. However, because of the variability of this species, it is often difficult to distinguish the sexes without dissection.

On hillsides, coasts, dry grasslands, roadsides and other dry places, chiefly on Lotus corniculatus *and possibly also on* L. tenuis. *Larvae in the pods. Widely distributed throughout the British Isles and generally very abundant; it is one of the commonest species of* Apion, *at least throughout England and Wales. Less general in Scotland, to W. Sutherland and Caithness, but not recorded from the Outer Hebrides, Orkney or Zetland. Widespread and common in Ireland. Probably throughout the Palaearctic.*

Subgenus **Oxystoma**

The strongly subulate and gibbous rostrum and the large and outstanding eyes characteristic of this group make it one of the most distinctive subgenera. Eleven species are known, all from the Palaearctic, with seven occurring in Europe and four in the British Isles. Differences between the three of these which are most easily confused were reviewed by Johnson (1965).

Key to species

1   Elytra and pronotum concolorous black, sometimes with an obscure metallic reflection; first elytral stria prolonged to base, or at least extending past the apex of the scutellum (fig. 253); pronotal furrow usually extending from base to well past middle (fig. 253); average size smaller, length 2·2–3·0 mm 2

—   Elytra distinctly blue, pronotum blue-black; first elytral stria normally not prolonged to base and usually not reaching the apex of the scutellum (fig. 252); pronotal furrow not usually extending far beyond middle, as long as, or shorter than, half of the length of the pronotum (fig. 252); average size larger, length 2·5–3·6 mm. [Penis neither dilated nor bent at apex (fig. 258)] . . . .**pomonae** (Fabricius)

Male with the rostrum shorter than the pronotum, narrowed less abruptly distally and much nearer apex (fig. 79), thickly pubescent almost to apex, dull; antennae inserted at about middle of rostrum. Female with the rostrum as long as pronotum, abruptly narrowed at about one-third from apex (evident in both dorsal and lateral views) (figs. 80, 87), sparsely pubescent, glabrous in distal third, shining; antennae inserted behind middle of rostrum.

On various species of Vicia *and* Lathyrus, *particularly* V. cracca, V. sepium *and* L. pratensis, *but range of foodplants not well known in Britain. Larvae in pods, feeding on the unripe seeds. Adults often on trees, especially in spring and autumn. Widely distributed and locally abundant in England northwards to Notts and Derbys. Recorded only from Merioneth in Wales. Records from northern England and from Scotland (Linlithgow, Renfrew) require confirmation. Not in Ireland. Europe through Asia to Siberia, N. Africa.*

2   Rostrum long, longer than, to almost as long as, pronotum, much less thickened and angled beneath (figs. 81, 82, 85, 86); eyes remote from antennal furrow, especially in female (figs. 82, 86); antennae with first two segments at most pitchy or obscurely yellowish, not clear yellow; size larger, 2·4–3·0 mm; [penis large, not greatly elongated, apex lobed (figs. 260, 261); spermatheca smoothly rounded at apex] 3

—   Rostrum short, distinctly shorter than pronotum, strongly thickened and angled beneath (figs. 83, 84); eyes close to antennal furrow (figs. 83, 84); antennae with at least first two segments clear yellow (entirely yellow in male, or sometimes reddish in female; size smaller, 2·2–2·6 mm; [penis small, narrow and elongated, curved dorsally, curved apically, without a distinct apical lobe (fig. 259); spermatheca bulging at apex] . . . .
. . . .**craccae** (Linnaeus)

Male with the rostrum thickly pubescent dorsally and almost to apex, shorter (fig. 83); antennae entirely clear yellow to reddish; body more thickly pubescent, especially ventrally. Female with the rostrum more sparsely pubescent dorsally and with the apical third narrow and shining, longer (fig. 84); antennae with the club and apical funicular segments black; body less thickly pubescent.

In hedgerows, wood edges, etc., frequently on trees and shrubs which are not food plants. Hosts are a wide variety of Vicia spp., and probably not other genera, but foodplants not well known in Britain. Larvae in pods, feeding on the seeds. Rather local, but widely distributed in England as far north as Northumberland South, though not recorded from many Midland vice-counties, and only from Glamorgan in Wales. No reliable Scottish records. Very local and uncommon in Ireland (N. and S. Kerry, Wicklow, Westmeath, Down). Europe, through Asia to Siberia; N. Africa.

3   Pronotum simply rounded at sides, almost rectangular in dorsal view, with the apical margin little narrower than the basal (fig. 253); basal segment of fore tarsi elongate and narrow, about $2\frac{1}{2} \times$ longer than broad (figs. 262, 263); rostrum longer, as long as, or longer than, the pronotum, gradually narrowed distad, much less subulate (figs. 85, 86); antennal scape narrow and longer, as long as, or longer than, the width of the rostrum at the antennal insertion, reddish yellow at base only. Length 2·4–3·0 mm; [penis simply dilated at apex (fig. 260)] . . . . **subulatum** Kirby

Male with the rostrum shorter, about as long as pronotum, gradually narrowed distad and pubescent nearly to apex (fig. 85). Female with the rostrum longer, evidently longer than the pronotum, narrower, apical part from the antennal insertion shining, glabrous (fig. 86).

In hedgerows and wood edges. The principal, perhaps exclusive, foodplant in Britain is Lathyrus pratensis. *Larvae in pods, feeding on the unripe seeds. Widely distributed and generally common throughout England and Wales. Distribution in Scotland uncertain because of confusion with A. (O.)* cerdo *but extending at least as far north as Forfar. Widely distributed in Ireland. Europe, Asia to Siberia, N. Africa.*

—   Pronotum constricted subapically and dilated at base, bell-shaped (fig. 266); basal segment of fore tarsi less elongate and broader, about $2 \times$ longer than broad (figs. 264, 265); rostrum shorter, evidently shorter than the pronotum, more abruptly narrowed distad, much more clearly and strongly subulate (figs. 81, 82); antennal scape broader, more robust, and shorter, not, or scarcely, as broad as rostrum at antennal insertion; more clearly yellow, darkened at apex only. Length 2·4–3·0 mm . . . . **cerdo** Gerstaecker

Male with the rostrum slightly shorter, less abruptly narrowed distad and pubescent almost to apex (fig. 81). Female with the rostrum a little longer, very abruptly narrowed distad (with the apical third almost tubular (fig. 82) and with the apex glabrous, strongly shining.

In hedgerows and waste places, on species of Vicia, *especially V.* cracca. *Larvae in the pods, feeding on the seeds. Local and not generally common, once regarded as exclusively, or almost exclusively, a species of northern England, Scotland and Ireland, but now known from some southern vice-counties (E. Sussex, E. and W. Kent, Hunts). Even in the north its range is very narrow: Durham, Northumberland South, Cumberland, Dumfries and Kirkcudbright only. Not recorded from the Lothians or northern Scotland, nor Wales. Widespread and apparently much more common in Ireland. Europe, through Asia to Mongolia and N.E. China.*

Subgenus **Protapion**

This group includes some familiar 'yellow-legged' species which are among the most abundant British *Apion*; several are pests of legumes, especially clover grown for seed. There has been much confusion in the determination of some species because of too much reliance on comparative, variable and inappropriate characters, but it must be admitted that the differences between some species are very slight and comparative. It is often useful, if not essential, to sex specimens; males may be distinguished from females because the pygidium is visible between the apices of the elytra when seen from behind. Of about 30 species in the Palaearctic region, 19 occur in Europe and 13 of these in the British Isles.

Key to species

1   Legs in part yellow, red or orange; antennae, at least at base, yellow, red or pitchy, sometimes obscurely so; [often larger species, 1·6–3·0 mm; on *Ononis* or *Trifolium* spp.] 2

— Legs and antennae entirely black; [small species, 1·5–2·0 mm; pronotum closely and rather finely punctured (fig. 267); rostrum weakly curved (fig. 267); on species of *Medicago*] . . . . **filirostre** Kirby

Male with the rostrum as long as, or a little shorter than, the head and pronotum combined, and with the antennae inserted in the middle. Female with the rostrum $1\frac{1}{2}$ × as long as the head and pronotum combined and with the antennae inserted a little behind the middle.

In dry grasslands and waste places, often on calcareous soils. Biology not well known in Britain though sometimes associated with Medicago lupulina, *but larvae on the continent in the buds of* Medicago sativa, M. falcata, M. media, *etc. Rather local, in southern England only, as far north as E. and W. Suffolk and Warwick but recorded from most of the southern counties. Not in Wales, Scotland or Ireland. Europe and Asia to Siberia.*

2 Hind tibiae with at least the distal half black or dark pitchy; [in teneral specimens some trace of this dark coloration can usually be seen]; legs somewhat darkened at the joint between tibia and femur 4

— Hind tibiae clear yellow or red throughout, except at extreme apex, where they are darkened; [all legs yellow or red]; legs not darkened at the joint between tibia and femur 3

3 Funiculus entirely yellow or red, at most with the distal segments a little darker; funicular segments 2–7 narrow, of equal width throughout, so club abruptly demarcated from funiculus, segments 6 and 7 elongate; antennal club short, about twice as long as broad (fig. 268); [fore coxae red or yellow in both sexes; male with rostrum red or yellow distally; on *Trifolium campestre, T. aureum* and *T. dubium* (yellow-flowered species); smaller and more delicate, 1·6–1·9 mm] . . . . **nigritarse** Kirby

Male with the rostrum red or yellow distally from insertion of the antennae, and about as long as the pronotum; antennae inserted at middle of rostrum. Female with the rostrum black throughout, a little longer than the pronotum; antennae inserted a little behind the middle of rostrum.

In grasslands and dry, open areas. Biology not well studied in Britain, but on the continent restricted to small, yellow-flowered species of Trifolium: T. campestre, T. dubium *and* T. aureum *(an introduced British species); larvae in the flowerheads. Fairly common throughout England and probably Wales (though records few), but in Scotland only in the south, as far north as Clyde Isles (Arran) and Peebles. Widely distributed but not common in Ireland. Europe, Asia to Siberia, and N. Africa.*

— Antennae with only the scape and first one or two funicular segments clear yellow or red, remaining segments darker, pitchy to black, becoming increasingly darker distally; funicular segments 2–7 robust, the distal ones progressively dilated, so club not so clearly demarcated from funiculus, segment 6 little longer than broad, 7 transverse; antennal club longer, about 3 × longer than broad (fig. 269); [fore coxae black in the female; on *Trifolium repens* and *T. hybridum* (white- or pink-flowered species); larger and more robust, 1·8–2·2 mm] . . . . **dichroum** Bedel

Male with fore coxae red; rostrum shorter, not as long as the pronotum and only just longer than the head, more robust and pubescent, and parallel-sided throughout; antennae inserted just in front of the middle of rostrum. Female with the fore coxae black; rostrum longer, much longer than the pronotum and nearly as long as the head and pronotum combined, more slender and shining, and slightly dilated at antennal insertion and apex; antennae inserted well behind the middle of the rostrum.

In grasslands, sandhills and all kinds of open places, also often adventitiously on trees and shrubs; on Trifolium repens *and* T. hybridum; *larvae in the flowerheads. Very abundant and almost ubiquitous throughout the British Isles, including the Outer Hebrides, Orkney and Zetland; it is the commonest and most widely distributed British species of* Apion *and is a pest of white clover (Freeman 1967). Throughout the Palaearctic region.*

4 Fore coxae entirely clear yellow or red; [red to pitchy in *A. (P.) schoenherri*; small species, 1·7–2·1 mm; male normal; pronotum finely punctured)] 5

— Fore coxae entirely black, or dark brown; [antennal scape as long as the first three funicular segments together, longer (about 1·25 ×) than the rostral width at insertion; male anomalous (see below); size large, 2·4–3·0 mm] . . . . **difforme** Germar

Male with many unusual characters; antennae with scape long and greatly dilated apically; funiculus with segments 1–6 flattened and expanded, 1 small, half as broad as apex of scape, 2 triangular, as broad as scape, 3 slightly elongate, as broad as scape, 4–6 much less broad, narrowing progressively distally, 7 elongate, not flattened; club hardly evident as such, segments little broader than funicular 7, and distinctly narrower than 2 and 3 (fig. 270);

rostrum robust, $1\frac{1}{2}\times$ broader at base than at apex, shorter than head and pronotum combined, antennae inserted in front of middle; fore tibiae strongly bisinuate (fig. 272), flattened on the external face and with a series of flat apical teeth; fore tarsus with segment 1 elongate, twisted and with a long, flat, inwardly-pointing, red tooth or flange (fig. 272), segment 2 slightly elongate, broad and flat; middle femur and, particularly, tibia abnormally long, the tibia longer than the rostrum; hind tibiae curved inwards and dilated gradually to apex, tarsal segment 1 flattened and slightly dilated apically, 2 flattened. Female normal; antennal segments narrow but cylindrical, club narrow but evident (fig. 271); rostrum subparallel, as long as, or a little longer than, the head and pronotum together; antennae inserted well behind middle of rostrum; legs normal.

In damp grasslands and marshes. Biology unknown; an association with Trifolium *spp. (Hoffmann 1958) seems more probable than one with* Polygonum hydropiper *(Fowler 1891). Locally common throughout southern England as far north as Warwick, Leicester and Notts. Recorded only from Glamorgan in Wales and not known from Scotland or Ireland. Western and southern Europe, N. Africa.*

5   Middle and hind tibiae bicoloured, basal half or third red or yellow, concolorous with the femora, or with a red or yellow sub-basal ring, the red or yellow and black portions clearly demarcated from each other (fig. 273).. 6

—   Middle and hind tibiae concolorous, black or at least dark brown or pitchy, if with a trace of red or yellow coloration then this darker than that of femora, obscure, and not clearly marked off from the darker coloration of the tibia 8

6   Pronotum deeply, coarsely and closely punctured, the punctures almost, or actually, confluent in places; head punctured or weakly striate between eyes, or with a U-shaped ridge and associated furrow (in male *A. dissimile*); rostrum slender, curved, narrower than the fore femora and distinctly longer than the pronotum; [smaller species, length 1·8–2·6 mm] 7

—   Pronotum shallowly, finely and diffusely punctured, the punctures never confluent or nearly so (fig. 274); head with two parallel, shallow longitudinal depressions between eyes separated by a furrow, or with three distinct striae (fig. 274); rostrum robust (fig. 274), almost straight, as broad as, or broader than, the fore femora and not, or only slightly, longer than the pronotum; a large and robust species, length 2·4–2·9 mm ...... **laevicolle** Kirby

Male with the rostrum slightly shorter, as long as the pronotum, with the apical half dull, antennae inserted in the middle; all coxae dentate. Female with the rostrum longer, a little longer than the pronotum, with the apical half shining, antennae inserted a little behind middle; coxae unarmed. However, the sexual differences are not marked.

Generally, but not exclusively, maritime, on cliffs and grasslands. Biology poorly known, but reputedly associated with Trifolium repens, *the larvae reported on the continent to live in galls on the plant. Southern maritime counties of England, and Surrey, from W. Cornwall to E. Suffolk only. Not in Scotland, Wales or Ireland. Mediterranean countries and N. Africa, mainly.*

7   Elytra long and slender, not strongly rounded at sides, about 1·6–1·7 × longer than broad (fig. 275); fore tibiae slightly expanded and produced inwards at apex (more strongly in male than female) (figs. 277, 278); antennal scape as long as, or at most only slightly longer than, the first two segments of the funiculus (fig. 279); segments of hind tarsi shorter and broader, the first only twice as long as broad; rostrum strongly curved, especially in female (fig. 280); length 2·2–2·6 mm; [male with antennae and tarsi normal] .... **varipes** Germar

Male with the fore tibiae more distinctly dilated and produced inwards at apex (fig. 277); rostrum shorter than the head and pronotum combined, broader and duller and less strongly curved; antennae inserted at, or a little in front of, the middle. Female with the fore tibiae only feebly dilated and produced inwards at apex (fig. 278); rostrum longer than the head and pronotum combined, narrower, particularly between antennal insertion and apex, strongly shining and very strongly curved (arched) (fig. 280); antennae inserted behind middle.

In grasslands, woodland edges and waste places. On Trifolium pratense *and possibly other clovers. Biology not well known in Britain and continental evidence contradictory; the larva feeds either in flowerheads or galls (Hoffmann 1958; but see Dieckmann 1977). Rather local, though sometimes abundant; recorded from most of southern England, from W. Cornwall and E. Kent northwards to S. Lincoln and Derby, with isolated occurrences in Durham, Kirkcudbright and Glamorgan. Otherwise not known from Wales or Scotland and absent from Ireland. Whole Palaearctic region.*

— Elytra short and broad, strongly rounded at sides, about 1·4–1·5 × longer than broad (fig. 276); fore tibiae straight, not expanded at apex in either sex (simple in female, emarginate in male (figs. 281, 282); antennal scape as long as, or a little longer than, the first four (male) or three (female) funicular segments (figs. 283, 284); segments of hind tarsi longer and narrower, the first 3 × longer than broad; rostrum less strongly curved (fig. 285); [length 1·8–2·3 mm; male with anomalous antennae and tarsi (see below)]. . . . .
. . . .**dissimile** Germar

   Male with the antennal scape clavate, dilated at apex; funicular segments 2–4 very short, 2 slightly elongate, 3 and 4 quadrate, these three segments together only as long as segment 5; segments 7 and 8 gradually dilated distad, broader than 1–6, so club not clearly marked off from remainder of funiculus (fig. 283); middle and hind tarsi with the segments expanded, depressed and rectangular; first and second segments of the fore tarsi produced at apex and base respectively to form a single, blunt, inwardly-pointing tooth (fig. 282); rostrum shorter than the head and pronotum together, dilated at base and at antennal insertion, which is at the middle; head between eyes with a U-shaped ridge and associated furrow. Female with the antennae, tarsi and head simple; funicular segments 7 and 8 only slightly dilated distad, so club more distinctly demarcated from funiculus (fig. 284); rostrum as long as, or slightly longer than, the head and pronotum together, weakly curved, with the antennae inserted behind middle, not strongly dilated here (dorsal view) and only very weakly at base but slightly flattened at junction with head (fig. 285).

   In dry, sparsely-vegetated, sandy places (but not on calcareous sands). On Trifolium arvense *only, the larvae in the inflorescences. Local and not common, but quite widely distributed. W. Cornwall, and Dorset to E. Kent northwards to Cambridge and E. Norfolk, and again in the north-west of England; Glamorgan and Merioneth, but not recorded from Scotland or Ireland. Europe and western Asia.*

8   Pronotum strongly, deeply and closely- to rugosely-punctured, basal fovea linear and at least moderately deep, somewhat variable in length but usually extending to at least middle of disc; pronotum moderately to slightly rounded at sides; fore coxae clear red or yellow; [mostly larger species, 2·0–2·9 mm; prothoracic coxae of male with or without a fine spine]. 9
— Pronotum finely, very shallowly but rather closely punctured; basal fovea indistinct, usually represented by a weak circular or oval depression and not extending to middle of disc (fig. 286); pronotum scarcely rounded at sides, subcylindrical (fig. 286); fore coxae red to light pitchy; smaller species, length 1·7–2·1 mm; [fore coxae of male without a fine spine; antennal segments without long, outstanding setae]. . . . .**schoenherri** Boheman

   Male with the rostrum shorter, only as long as the pronotum, or a very little longer, weakly curved (almost straight) (fig. 287) and strongly narrowed distad; antennae inserted at middle, more robust, funicular segments only slightly longer than broad, excepting segment 5, which is longer than any other segment, at least twice as long as broad and nearly as long as the scape (fig. 289); pronotum more distinctly cylindrical. Female with the rostrum longer, as long as, or little shorter than, the head and pronotum combined, evidently but not strongly curved (fig. 288) and cylindrical, not narrowed distad; antennae inserted behind middle; longer and less robust, funicular segments distinctly elongate, about twice as long as broad, segment 5 not longer than any of the preceding four and little longer than 6 or 7 (fig. 290); pronotum less clearly subcylindrical, somewhat broader at base than at apex.

   In grassy and open places, particularly, but not exclusively, near the coast. Probably on species of Trifolium, *but biology unknown. Very local and scarce. Southern England from S. Devon and E. Kent northwards to Oxford, Berks, Herts and S. Essex; also recorded from N.E. Yorks. Not recorded from Wales, Scotland or Ireland. Southern and eastern Europe and Mediterranean countries to Syria, Asia Minor and the Ukraine.*

9   Trochanters red or yellow, concolorous with femora, at most with darker margins; pronotum distinctly longer than broad; size larger, length 1·8–2·9 mm 10
— Trochanters black, brown or pitchy, darker than the femora; pronotum generally less distinctly longer than broad, or quadrate (but variable) (fig. 291); size smaller, length 1·7–2·1 mm; [antennae short, funicular segments 4–7 only a little longer than broad, without long, outstanding setae (fig. 292); male with fore coxae unarmed]. . . . .
. . . .**trifolii** (Linnaeus)
   A variable and polymorphic species, with several sibling species on the continent, none of which has been recorded from the British Isles. Male with the rostrum shorter than the head and pronotum together, very slightly narrowed distad, antennae inserted at, or a little behind,

62

*the middle (fig. 293). Female with the rostrum longer than the head and pronotum together,
cylindrical, antennae inserted distinctly behind middle (fig. 294).*
    In grasslands, hedgerows and waste places. On Trifolium pratense *and* T. medium *but not
(on the continent, at least) on* T. repens *or* T. hybridum; *larvae in the flowerheads. Widely
distributed and abundant throughout England and Wales but recorded only from Dumfries in
Scotland. A pest of red clover. Rare in Ireland; recorded only from E. Cork and Kilkenny.
Europe, Asia, N. Africa.*

10   Rostrum shorter than head and pronotum combined (figs. 295–297, 301–304), slightly
    narrowed distad from antennal insertion; antennae inserted at, or slightly in front of,
    middle. Fore coxae with a very fine spine which points downwards and slightly inwards
    (fig. 307); [this spine is absent in male *A. apricans*] ....(males) 11
—   Rostrum longer than, or as long as, head and pronotum combined, cylindrical throughout
    (figs. 298–300); antennae inserted behind middle. Fore coxae unarmed ..... (females) 14

11   Rostrum more strongly curved (figs. 295, 296); fore coxae armed with a fine spine (fig. 307,
    couplet 10); pronotum deeply and strongly- to rugosely-punctured, punctures confluent,
    particularly at sides 12
—   Rostrum less strongly curved, straighter (fig. 297); fore coxae unarmed; pronotum distinctly
    but shallowly punctured, punctures not confluent, at least at middle of sides ....
    .... (see below) **apricans** (Herbst)

12   Rostrum more distinctly narrowed distad (fig. 301), antennae with segments of funiculus
    bearing long, outstanding setae, some as long as, or longer than, a segment (fig. 306);
    antennae longer, without club longer than rostrum; scape indistinctly, but not strongly,
    dilated distad, evidently broader than the next segment (fig. 306); head distinctly narrowed
    behind eyes; pronotum narrow, scarcely rounded at sides (fig. 301); [on *Ononis*] ....
    .... (see below) **ononicola** Bach
—   Rostrum not, or less distinctly, narrowed distad (figs. 302–304); if funicular segments of
    antennae with outstanding setae, these shorter, not as long as the length of a segment
    (fig. 305); antennae shorter, without club shorter than, or only as long as, rostrum; scape
    simple, not dilated distad, not broader than the next segment (fig. 305); head not, or
    less distinctly, narrowed behind eyes; pronotum broader, evidently rounded at sides (figs.
    302–304): [on *Trifolium*] 13

13   Pronotum narrower and more elongate, 1·05–1·08 × longer than broad (fig. 303), more
    closely and strongly punctured, the punctures somewhat confluent in front of the disc;
    head narrower, with the eyes a little less prominent ....(see below) **assimile** Kirby
—   Pronotum broader and less elongate, 1·00–1·01 × longer than broad (fig. 304), less closely
    and not so strongly punctured, the punctures not, or scarcely, confluent in front of disc;
    head broader, with the eyes rather more prominent; [so far recorded from Zetland, Orkney
    and Outer Hebrides only] .... (see below) **ryei** Blackburn

14   Rostrum longer and straighter, 1·2–1·3 × longer than head and pronotum combined (fig.
    298); pronotum distinctly, but shallowly, much less strongly, and somewhat more diffusely
    punctured, punctures not confluent at sides...................... **apricans** (Herbst)
    Sexual differences as in key.
    In grasslands, waste places and clover fields. On Trifolium pratense, *and probably only on
this species. A pest of red clover. Larvae in the flowerheads. Abundant and widely distributed
throughout England, Wales and Ireland. Probably equally abundant in Scotland but
recorded only from Dumfries, Kirkcudbright, Berwick, Edinburgh, the Ebudes, Outer
Hebrides and W. Sutherland. All the Palaearctic region.*
—   Rostrum shorter and more curved, 1·0–1·15 × longer than head and pronotum combined
    (figs. 299, 300); pronotum more strongly, deeply and more closely punctured, the
    punctures confluent at sides (and often also on disc) 15

15   Funiculus with longer, more evidently outstanding setae, some setae longer than the segment
    bearing them (fig. 308); pronotum more elongate, 1·10–1·15 × longer than broad, and
    narrower in proportion to elytra, more rugosely and confluently punctured; [on *Ononis*] .
    .... **ononicola** Bach
    *Sexual differences as in key. The apical dilation of the antennal scape in the male is
particularly distinctive.*
    *In grassy, open places; particularly, but by no means exclusively, coastal, on sandhills and
cliffs. On* Ononis repens *and* O. spinosa. *Larvae in fruits, one, or less often, two to a fruit.
Widely distributed and locally abundant in England and Wales as far north as N.E. and N.W.
(?) Yorks. Also recorded from Kirkcudbright, Ayr and N. Ebudes (Rhum), but Scottish*

records requiring clarification. Irish records (W. Donegal, etc.) also needing confirmation. Europe, W. Asia and N. Africa.

— Funiculus with shorter, less evidently outstanding setae, of which none, or only one or two, is as long as the segment bearing it (figs. 309, 310); pronotum less elongate, $1\cdot02$–$1\cdot08 \times$ longer than broad, and broader in proportion to the elytra, less rugosely and confluently punctured; [on *Trifolium*] 16

16 Pronotum slightly narrower and more elongate, $1\cdot04$–$1\cdot08 \times$ longer than broad, a little more closely and strongly punctured, punctures more confluent at sides and on anterior part of disc; head a little narrower; [common and widely distributed] .... **assimile** Kirby
   Sexual differences as in key; there are no striking distinctions, save the male prothoracic coxal spine and the difference in the length of the rostrum.
   In grasslands, waste places, verges, wood edges, etc. On species of Trifolium; recorded on the continent from T. pratense, T. medium, T. hybridum and T. ochroleucon. Larvae in the flowerheads. Abundant and widely distributed throughout England and Wales. Apparently less common in Scotland, but paucity of records undoubtedly due, in part, to confusion with other species; widely distributed from Dumfries to W. Sutherland, and also recorded from S. and N. Ebudes and Zetland. In Ireland definitely recorded only from Antrim. The whole Palaearctic region.

— Pronotum slightly broader and less elongate, $1\cdot02$–$1\cdot05 \times$ longer than broad, slightly less closely and less strongly punctured, punctures less confluent at sides and on anterior part of disc; head broader, especially behind; [Outer Hebrides, Orkney and Zetland only] ....
   .... **ryei** Blackburn
   The slight and very comparative characters which distinguish this taxon from *A. assimile* reflect considerable doubt as to its specific distinctness. It may fall within the range of variation of *A. assimile sensu lato,* and be part of a roughly north–south geographical cline. *A. ryei* is retained here as a species pending a thorough revision of the British *Protapion*.
   Sexual differences as in A. assimile.
   On roadsides and in waste places. On Trifolium pratense, probably exclusively. The larvae probably feed in the flowerheads. Recorded only from the Outer Hebrides, Orkney and Zetland and not known outside the British Isles.

Subfamily Nanophyinae

The genus *Nanophyes* Schoenherr is the sole representative of this subfamily.

Genus **Nanophyes** Schoenherr

This genus is rich in species in the southern Palaearctic, Afrotropical, Malagasy, Oriental and Australasian regions or subregions. Even in France, 24 species have been recorded, but only two are known from the British Isles. Both our species are associated with Lythraceae.

Key to species

1 All the femora armed underneath with two sharp spines, the outer one smaller than the inner (fig. 311); rostrum longer and less robust (fig. 312), in the female as long as, or longer than, in the male a little shorter than, the head and pronotum together; legs a little longer and less robust; antennae with the first segment of the funiculus less rounded at sides and longer, about $2\cdot5 \times$ longer than broad, club longer, especially the last segment, which is twice as long as broad (fig. 313); [male with the apical teeth of the tibiae longer and more distinct and with the hind tibiae bowed]. Length $0\cdot7$–$1\cdot9$ mm ..... **gracilis** Redtenbacher
   Male with all the tibiae armed apically with a distinct, slender, pointed tooth (more obvious on fore and hind tibiae than middle ones) (cf. fig. 317); hind tibia strongly bent inwards; rostrum shorter, not, or scarcely, as long as the head and pronotum combined, duller

distad; antennae inserted at about one-third from apex. Female with the tibiae unarmed (cf. fig. 318); hind tibia simple, straight, not strongly bent inwards; rostrum longer, as long as, or a little longer than, the head and pronotum combined, more shining distad; antennae inserted at about 0·45 from apex.

In wet or damp, muddy places, often near or under trees. On Lythrum portula; the larvae in galls on secondary stems. Very local and generally rare, southern England only: Dorset, Isle of Wight, N. and S. Hants, E. and W. Sussex, Surrey and Berks. Not recorded from Wales, Scotland or Ireland. Southern and mid-Europe, N. Africa.

— All the femora simple, unarmed (fig. 314); rostrum shorter and more robust, in the female not quite as long as the head and pronotum combined (fig. 315), in the male only as long as the pronotum and half the head together; legs a little shorter and more robust; antennae with the first segment of the funiculus more rounded at sides and shorter, only twice as long as broad, club shorter, the last segment a little less than twice as long as broad (fig. 316); [male with the apical teeth of the tibiae shorter and less distinct and with the hind tibiae not bowed]. Length 1·0–2·0 mm. . . . . **marmoratus** Goeze (fig. 321)

Male with all the tibiae armed apically with a small tooth (most easily seen on the fore and hind tibiae) (fig. 317); rostrum shorter, only as long as the pronotum combined with half the length of the head, duller distad; antennae inserted nearer base of rostrum, at 0·37–0·42 from apex. Female with all the tibiae unarmed (fig. 318); rostrum longer, not quite as long as the head and pronotum combined, more shining distad; antennae inserted nearer base of rostrum, at 0·43–0·48 from apex.

In fens and marshes and by banks of streams, rivers and canals. On Lythrum salicaria; the larvae in the ovaries. Widely distributed, common, and often abundant throughout most of England and Wales. Distribution in Scotland greatly restricted by the absence of the host-plant from the north and east, but recorded from Kirkcudbright, Clyde Isles and S. Ebudes. Widespread and common in Ireland. All Europe to Siberia.

References

ALFORD, D. V. 1984. *Fruit pests: their recognition, biology and control.* Wolf Publishing, London.

ALLEN, A. A. 1964. On the synonymy of *Rhynchites sericeus* Hbst., *ophthalmicus* Steph. and *olivaceus* Gyll. (Col., Attelabidae). *Entomologist's mon. Mag.* **100**: 44.

ASLAM, N. A. 1961. An assessment of some internal characters in the higher classification of the Curculionidae s.l. (Coleoptera). *Trans. R. ent. Soc. Lond.* **115**: 417–489.

BRANDL, P. 1981. Familie Bruchidae (Samenkäfer). *In:* Freude, H., Harde, K. W. & Lohse, G. A. *Die Käfer Mitteleuropas* **10**: 7–21.

COCKBAIN, A. J., BOWEN, R. & BARTLETT, P. W. 1982. Observations on the biology and ecology of *Apion vorax* (Col., Apionidae) a vector of broad bean stain and broad bean true mosaic viruses. *Ann. appl. Biol.* **101**: 449–457.

CLAPHAM, A. R., TUTIN, T. G. & MOORE, D. M. 1987. *Flora of the British Isles* (3rd ed.). Cambridge University Press, Cambridge.

COOPE, G. R. 1970. Interpretations of quaternary insect-fossils. *A. Rev. Ent.* **15**: 97–120.

CROWSON, R. A. 1950–54. The classification of the families of British Coleoptera. *Entomologist's mon. Mag.* **86–90**: *passim.*

CROWSON, R. A. 1956. Coleoptera. Introduction and keys to families. *Handbk Ident. Br. Insects* **4**(1): 1–59.

CROWSON, R. A. 1967. *The natural classification of the families of Coleoptera* (reprint with addenda et corrigenda). E. W. Classey, Hampton.

CROWSON, R. A. 1984. On the systematic position of *Bruchela* Dejean (*Urodon* auctt.) (Coleoptera). *Coleopt. Bull.* **38**: 91–93.

CROWSON, R. A. 1985. The systematic position of *Nemonyx* Redtenbacher (Col.). *Entomologist's mon. Mag.* **121**: 144.

CYMOREK, S. 1963. Über die Biologie und den Genitalbau des Zwergbreitrüsslers *Choragus sheppardi* Kirby (Col., Anthribidae). *Ent. Bl. Biol. Syst. Käfer* **59**: 151–161.

DANDY, J. E. 1969. *Watsonian vice-counties of Great Britain.* Ray Society, London.

DAVIES, W. M. 1928. The bionomics of *Apion ulicis* Först. (Gorse weevil), with special reference to its rôle in the control of *Ulex europaeus* in New Zealand. *Ann. appl. Biol.* **15**: 263–285.

DAY, F. H. 1915. A Cumberland nature reserve. Coleoptera. *Naturalist, Hull* **40:** 238–243.
DIECKMANN, L. 1972. Beiträge zur Insektenfauna der DDR: Coleoptera — Curculionidae: Ceutorhynchinae. *Beitr. Ent.* **22:** 3–128.
DIECKMANN, L. 1973. *Apion*-Studien (Coleoptera: Curculionidae). *Beitr. Ent.* **23:** 71–92.
DIECKMANN, L. 1974. Beiträge zur Insektenfauna der DDR: Coleoptera — Curculionidae (Rhinomacerinae, Rhynchitinae, Attelabinae, Apoderinae). *Beitr. Ent.* **24:** 5–54.
DIECKMANN, L. 1976. Revision der *Apion platalea*-Gruppe (Coleoptera, Curculionidae). *Ent. Nachr.* **20:** 117–128.
DIECKMANN, L. 1977. Beiträge zur Insektenfauna der DDR: Coleoptera — Curculionidae (Apioninae). *Beitr. Ent.* **27:** 7–143.
DIECKMANN, L. 1980. Beiträge zur Insektenfauna der DDR: Coleoptera — Curculionidae (Brachycerinae, Otiorhynchinae, Brachyderinae). *Beitr. Ent.* **30:** 145–310.
DOLLING, W. R. 1975. The first record of *Apion dispar* Germar (Col., Curculionidae) in Britain. *Entomologist's mon. Mag.* **110**(1974): 181.
DUFFY, E. A. J. 1953. Coleoptera. Scolytidae and Platypodidae. *Handbk Ident. Br. Insects* **5**(15): 1–20.
EASTON, A. M. 1946. *Apion lemoroi* Brisout (Col., Curculionidae) a species new to Britain. *Entomologist's mon. Mag.* **82:** 130–131.
EMDEN, F. I. van 1938. On the taxonomy of *Rhynchophora* larvae (Coleoptera). *Trans. R. ent. Soc. Lond.* **87:** 1–37.
EMDEN, F. I. van 1952. On the taxonomy of *Rhynchophora* larvae: Adelognatha and Alophinae (Insecta: Coleoptera). *Proc. zool. Soc. Lond.* **122:** 651–795.
FISHER, J. P. 1970. The biology and taxonomy of some chalcidoid parasites (Hymenoptera) of stem-living larvae of *Apion* (Coleoptera: Curculionidae). *Trans. R. ent. Soc. Lond.* **122:** 293–322.
FOWLER, W. W. 1891. *The Coleoptera of the British Islands* **5**. L. Reeve, London.
FOWLER, W. W. & DONISTHORPE, H. St. J. 1913. *The Coleoptera of the British Islands* **6**. L. Reeve, Ashford.
FREEMAN, B. E. 1967. The biology of the white clover seed weevil, *Apion dichroum* Bedel (Col., Curculionidae). *J. appl. Ecol.* **4:** 535–552.
FREUDE, H., HARDE, K. W. & LOHSE, G. A. 1981. *Die Käfer Mitteleuropas* **10:** 1–310, Goecke & Evers, Krefeld.
FREUDE, H., HARDE, K. W. & LOHSE, G. A. 1983. *Die Käfer Mitteleuropas* **11:** 1–342, Goecke & Evers, Krefeld.
HARDE, K. W. (ed. HAMMOND, P. M.) 1984. *A Field Guide in Colour to Beetles* 1–334. Octopus Books, London.
HOFFMANN, A. 1945. Coléoptères Bruchides et Anthribides. *Faune de France* **44:** 1–184. Paul Lechevalier, Paris.
HOFFMANN, A. 1950. Coléoptères Curculionides (1re partie). *Faune de France* **52:** 1–486. Paul Lechevalier, Paris.
HOFFMANN, A. 1954. Coléoptères Curculionides (2me partie). *Faune de France* **59:** 487–1208. Libraire de la Faculté des Sciences, Paris.
HOFFMANN, A. 1958. Coléoptères Curculionides (3me partie). *Fauna de France* **62:** 1209–1829. Libraire de la Faculté des Sciences, Paris.
JOHNSON, C. 1965. Taxonomic notes on British Coleoptera. 1. *Apion cerdo* and its allies (Apionidae). *Entomologist* **98:** 80–82.
JOY, N. H. 1932. *A Practical Handbook of British Beetles* (2 vols.). H. F. & G. Witherby, London.
KISSINGER, D. G. 1968. *Curculionidae subfamily Apioninae of North and Central America. With reviews of the world genera of Apioninae and world subgenera of Apion Herbst. (Coleoptera)*. Taxonomic Publications, South Lancaster, Mass.
KLOET, G. S. & HINCKS, W. D. 1945. *A Check List of British Insects*. Kloet & Hincks, Stockport.
KLOET, G. S. & HINCKS, W. D. 1977. A check list of British insects (2nd ed.) Coleoptera. *Handbk Ident. Br. Insects* **11**(3): 1–105.
LOHSE, G. A. 1981. Unterfamilien Rhinomacerinae, Rhynchitinae, Attelabinae, Apoderinae und Apioninae. *In:* Freude, H., Harde, K. W. & Lohse, G. A. *Die Käfer Mitteleuropas* **10:** 112–183.
MASSEE, A. M. 1954. *The Pests of Fruit and Hops* 3rd (revised) ed. Crosby Lockwood, London.

MORIMOTO, K. 1962. Comparative morphology and phylogeny of the superfamily Curculionoidea of Japan (Comparative morphology, phylogeny and systematics of the superfamily Curculionoidea of Japan, I.). *J. Fac. Agric. Kyushu Univ.* **11:** 331–373.

MORIMOTO, K. 1976. Notes on the family characters of Apionidae and Brentidae (Coleoptera), with key to the related subfamilies. *Kontyû* **44:** 469–476.

MORLEY, C. 1941. *Apion armatum* Gerst. (Col., Curculionidae), new to Britain, in the New Forest. *Entomologist's mon. Mag.* **77:** 133–134.

MORRIS, M. G. 1976a. *Apion sicardi* Desbrochers, a species of weevil (Col., Apionidae) new to Britain. *Entomologist's mon. Mag.* **111**(1975): 165–171.

MORRIS, M. G. 1976b. An introduction to the biology of weevils. *Trans. Proc. Brit. ent. nat. Hist. Soc.* **9:** 66–82.

MORRIS, M. G. 1983. Dorset weevils (Coleoptera, Curculionoidea): additional, critical and notable species 1968–1982. *Proc. Dorset nat. Hist. archaeol. Soc.* **104:** 159–164.

PARRY, J. 1962. The genus *Apion* Herbst and some other notable weevils in East Kent. *Entomologist's Rec. J. Var.* **74:** 267–272.

PARRY, J. A. 1982. A weevil new to Britain: *Apion intermedium* Eppelsheim (Col., Curculionidae) in Kent. *Entomologist's mon. Mag.* **118:** 227–229.

SCHERF, H. 1964. Die Entwicklungsstadien der mitteleuropäischen Curculioniden (Morphologie, Bionomie, Ökologie). *Abh. senckenb. naturf. Ges.* **506:** 1–335.

SOUTHWOOD, T. R. E. 1978. *Ecological Methods; with Particular Reference to the Study of Insect Populations* (2nd ed.). Methuen, London.

STEPHENS, J. F. 1831. *Illustrations of British Entomology. Mandibulata* **4:** Baldwin & Cradock, London.

STEPHENS, J. F. 1839. *A Manual of British Coleoptera.* Longman, London.

THOMPSON, R. T. & ALONSO-ZARAZAGA, M. A. 1988. On some weevil species described by Linnaeus (Coleoptera, Curculionoidea). *Ent. scand.* **19:** 81–86.

UNWIN, D. M. 1984. A key to the families of British Coleoptera (and Strepsiptera). *Field Studies* **6:** 149–197.

VOSS, E. 1932. Monographie der Rhynchiten-Tribus Rhynchitini, 2. Gattungsgruppen Rhynchitina. *Koleopt. Rdsch.* **18:** 153–189.

WAGNER, H. 1930. Apioninae. In: Winkler, A. *Catalogus Coleopterorum Regionis Palaearticae* pars. **11:** 1385–1391.

WALSH, G. B. & DIBB, J. R. (eds.) 1975. *A Coleopterist's Handbook* (2nd ed., revised Cooter, J. & Cribb, P. W.). Amateur Entomologists' Society, London.

WALTON, J. 1844. Notes on the synonymy of the genus *Apion* with descriptions of five new species, etc. *Ann. Mag. nat. Hist.* **13:** 444–457.

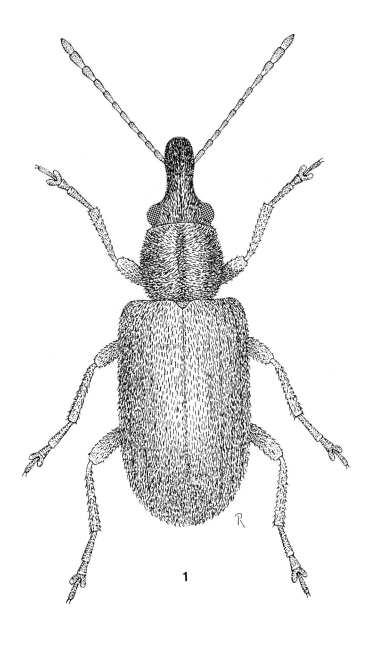

Fig. 1. *Cimberis attelaboides*, female.

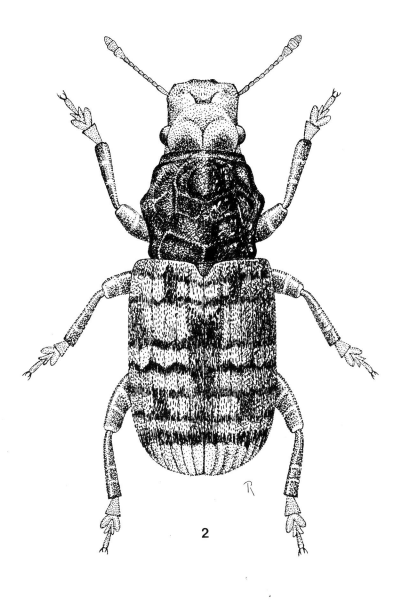

Fig. 2. *Platyrhinus resinosus*, female.

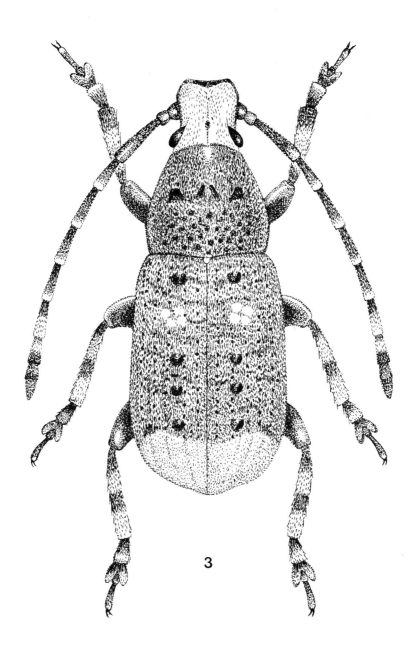

3

Fig. 3. *Platystomos albinus*, male.

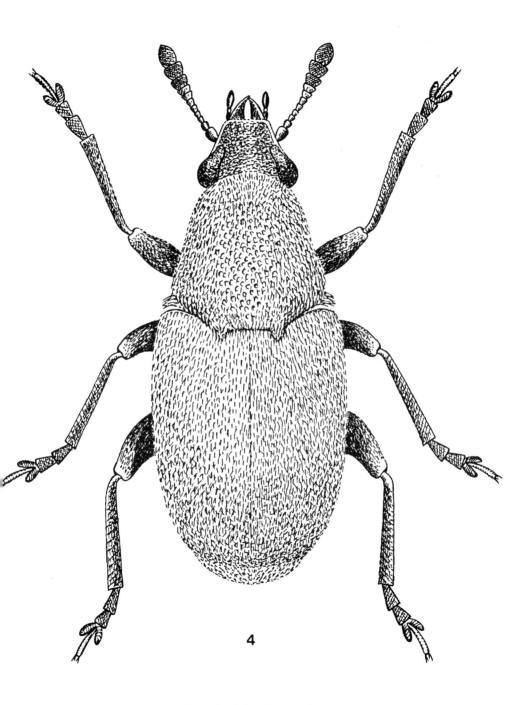

4

Fig. 4. *Bruchela rufipes*, female.

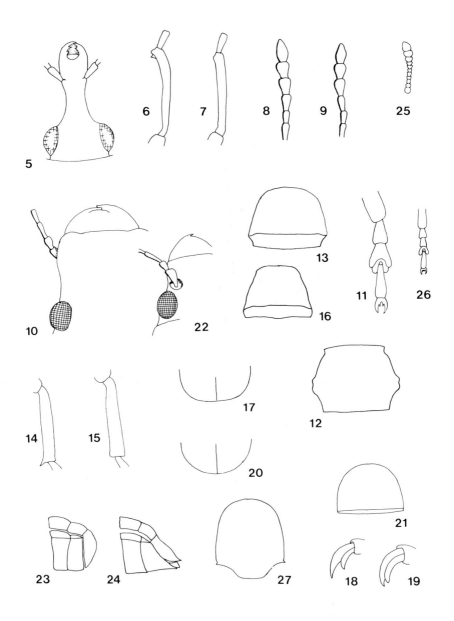

Figs 5–27. Nemonychidae, Anthribidae and Urodontidae. 5–9, *Cimberis attelaboides,* 5, head, dorsal view. 6, fore tibia, male. 7, do., female. 8, antennal apex, male. 9, do., female. 10–12, *Platyrhinus resinosus,* 10, left side of head, dorsal view. 11, hind tarsus. 12, outline of pronotum. 13–15, *Tropideres niveirostris,* 13, pronotum. 14, hind tibia, male. 15, hind tibia, female. 16, *T. sepicola,* pronotum. 17–19, *Anthribus fasciatus,* 17, apex of elytra. 18, fore tarsal claws, male. 19, do., female. 20, *A. nebulosus,* apex of elytra. 21, *Choragus sheppardi,* pronotum. 22–24, *Araecerus fasciculatus,* 22, left side of head. 23, abdomen, left side, male. 24, do., female. 25–27, *Bruchela rufipes,* 25, antenna. 26, hind tarsus. 27, outline of pronotum.

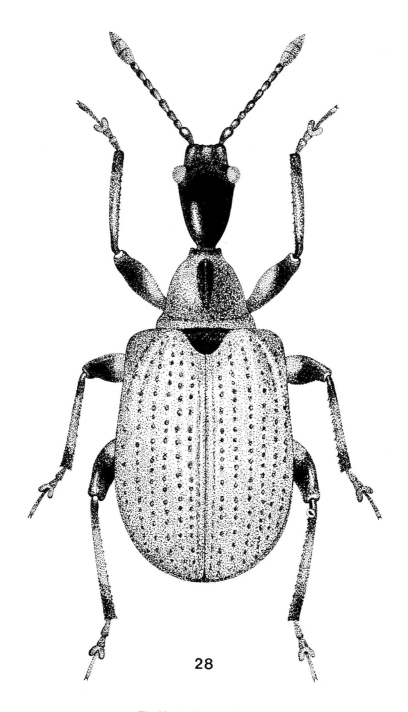

28

Fig. 28. *Apoderus coryli*, male.

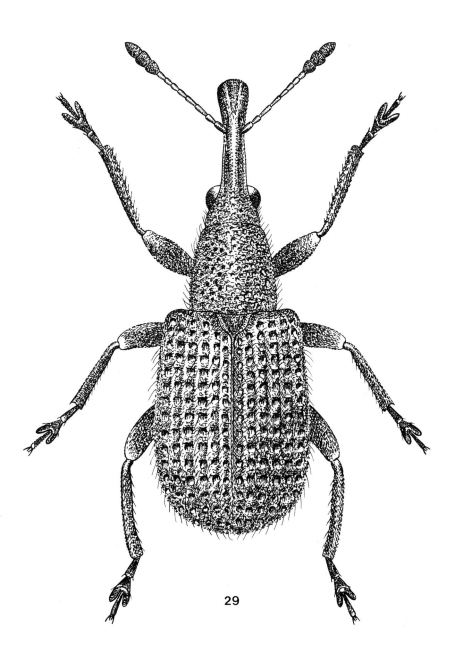

29

Fig. 29. *Rhynchites cupreus*, male.

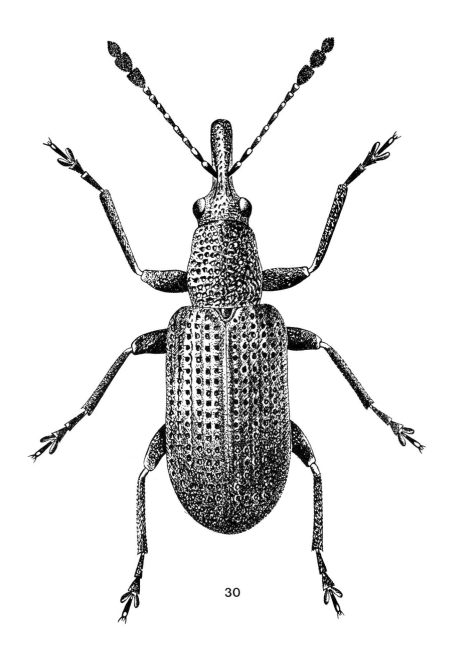

30

Fig. 30. *Rhynchites nanus*, male.

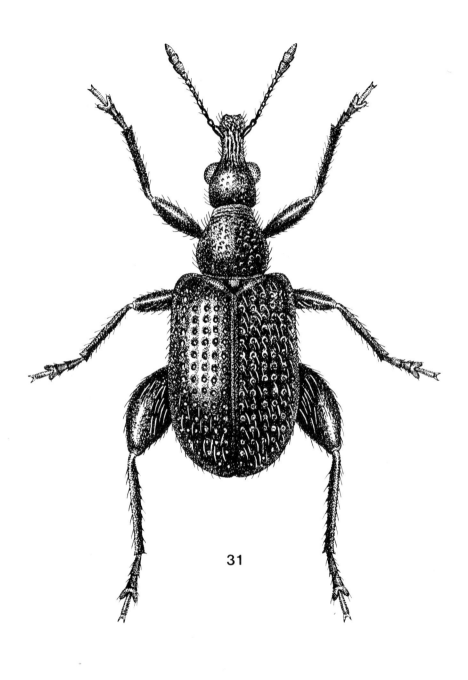

31

Fig. 31. *Deporaus betulae*, male.

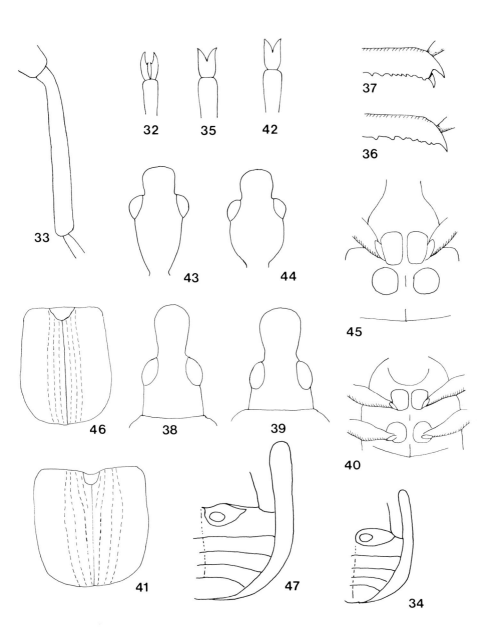

Figs 32–47. Attelabidae. 32–34, *Rhynchites (Lasiorhynchites) cavifrons,* 32, tarsal claws. 33, tibia. 34, hind coxae and abdomen from below. 35–41, *Attelabus nitens.* 35, tarsal claws. 36, tibial apex of male. 37, tibial apex of female. 38, head of male. 39, head of female. 40, fore and middle coxae from below. 41, elytra. 42–46, *Apoderus coryli,* 42, tarsal claws. 43, head of male. 44, head of female. 45, fore and middle coxae from below. 46, elytra. 47, *Byctiscus betulae,* hind coxae and abdomen from below.

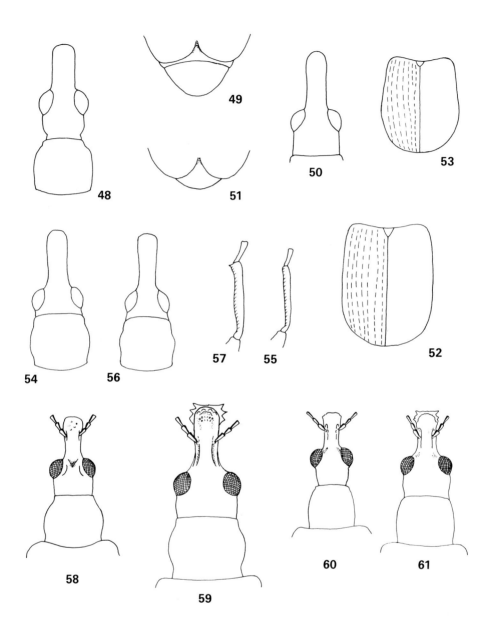

Figs 48–61. Attelabidae. 48–49, *Deporaus betulae,* 48, head. 49, pygidium. 50–52, *Rhynchites* (s.str.) *cupreus,* 50, head. 51, pygidium. 52, elytra. 53, *R. (Neocoenorrhinus) germanicus,* elytra. 54–55, *R. (Pselaphorynchites) nanus,* 54, head and pronotum of male. 55, fore tibia. 56, *R. (P.) longiceps,* head and pronotum of male. 57, *R. (P.) tomentosus,* fore tibia. 58–59, *R. (Lasiorhynchites) cavifrons,* 58, head and pronotum of male. 59, do., female. 60–61, *R. (L.) olivaceus.* 60, head and pronotum of male. 61, do., female.

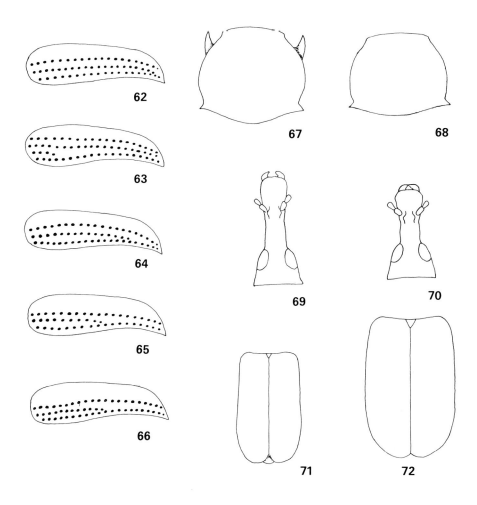

Figs 62–72. Attelabidae. 62–66, right elytra of *Rhynchites (Neocoenorrhinus)* spp. from side. 62, *aeneovirens*. 63, *germanicus*. 64, *interpunctatus*. 65, *pauxillus*. 66, *aequatus*. 67–68, *Byctiscus betulae*. 67, pronotum of male. 68, do., female. 69–70, *B. populi*. 69, head of male. 70, do., female. 71, *Deporaus mannerheimi*, elytra of male. 72, *D. betulae*, elytra of male.

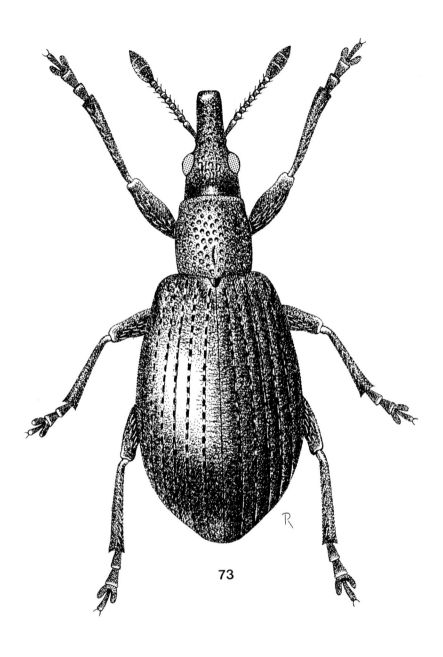

73

Fig. 73. *Apion hydrolapathi,* female.

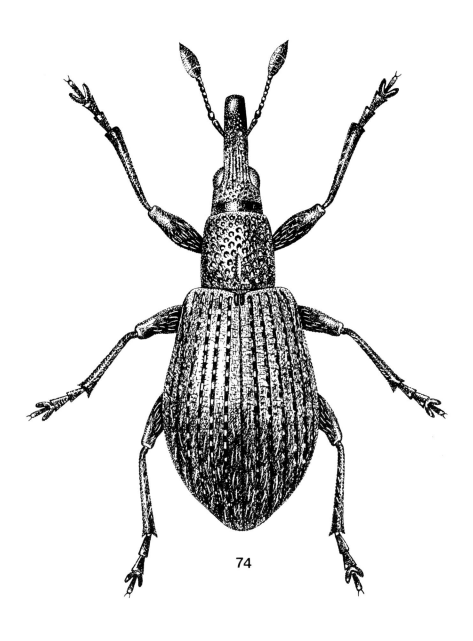

74

Fig. 74. *Apion curtirostre*, female.

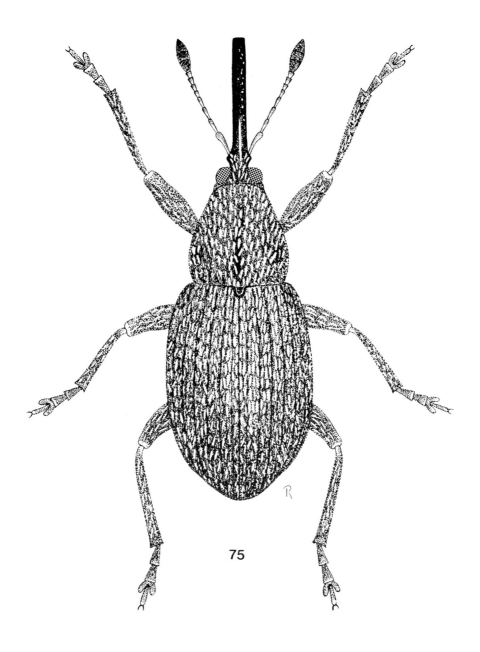

75

Fig. 75. *Apion ulicis*, female.

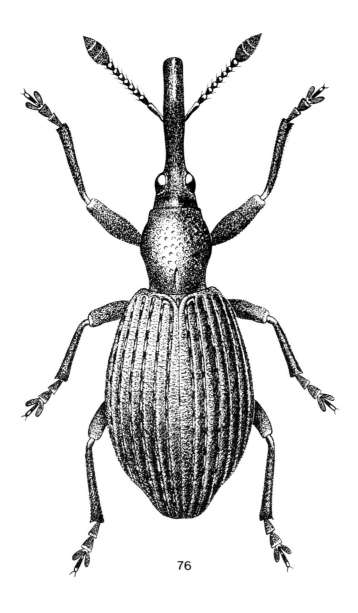

76

Fig. 76. *Apion ebeninum*, female.

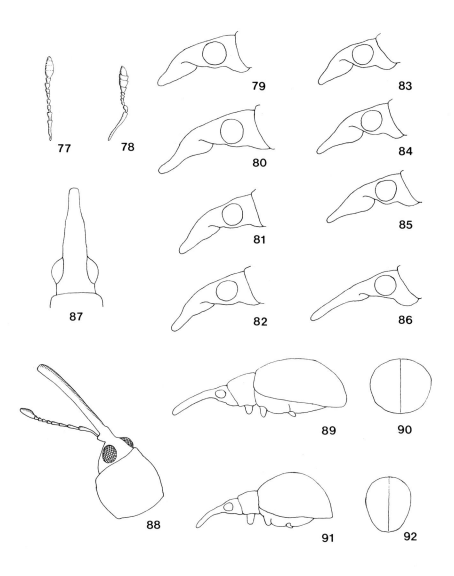

Figs 77–92. Apionidae. 77, *Apion (Pirapion) atratulum* (Apioninae), right antenna. 78, *Nanophyes marmoratus* (Nanophyinae), right antenna. 79–86, *Apion (Oxystoma)* spp., heads in profile. 79, *pomonae*, male. 80, *pomonae*, female. 81, *cerdo*, male. 82, *cerdo*, female. 83, *craccae*, male. 84, *craccae*, female. 85, *subulatum*, male. 86, *subulatum*, female. 87, *A. (O.) pomonae*, female head from above. 88, *A. (Exapion) ulicis*, female head in dorso-lateral view. 89–90, *A. (Pseudapion) rufirostre*, body in profile and cross-section. 91–92, *A. (Protapion) dichroum*, body in profile and cross-section.

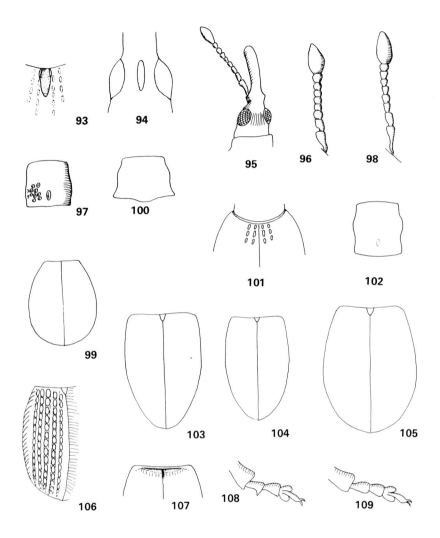

Figs 93–109. *Apion* spp. 93, *A. (Aspidapion) radiolus,* scutellum showing basal carinae. 94, *A. (A.) aeneum,* head from above. 95, *A. (Ceratapion) carduorum,* male head in dorso-lateral view. 96–97, *A. (C.) onopordi.* 96, right antenna of male. 97, male pronotum, showing part of puncturation. 98–99, *A. (Pirapion) atratulum.* 98, right antenna of male. 99, outline of male elytra. 100, *A. (Thymapion) vicinum,* outline of male pronotum. 101–102, *A. (Synapion) ebeninum,* 101, base of female elytra. 102, outline of pronotum. 103, *A. (Catapion) pubescens,* outline of male elytra. 104, *A. (C.) seniculus,* outline of male elytra. 105, *A. (Eutrichapion) reflexum,* outline of male elytra. 106, *A. (Melanapion) minimum,* part of female elytra in dorso-lateral view showing striae. 107, *A. (Perapion) limonii,* base of elytra. 108–109, *A. (P.) violaceum.* 108, male hind tarsus (showing tooth). 109, female hind tarsus (without tooth). (Figures of elytra not to scale.)

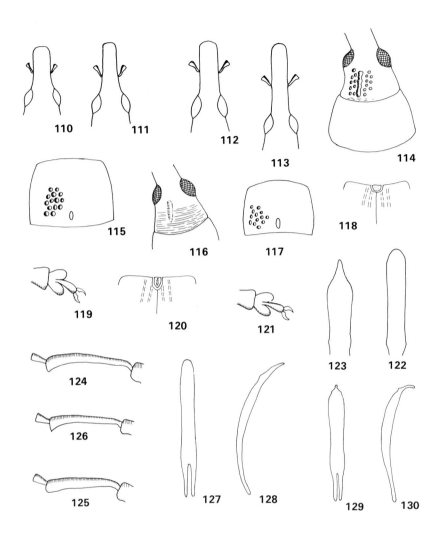

Figs 110–130. *Apion* spp. 110–111, *A. (Perapion) hydrolapathi.* 101, head of male. 111, do., female. 112–113, *A. (P.) violaceum.* 112, head of male. 113, do., female. 114–115, *A. (P.) affine.* 114, underside of male head, ventro-lateral view. 115, pronotum, with detail of puncturation. 116–117, *A. (P.) marchicum.* 116, underside of male head, ventro-lateral view. 117, pronotum, with detail of puncturation. 118–119, *A. (P.) sedi.* 118, base of elytra and scutellum. 119, tarsal claws, showing teeth. 120–122, *A. (P.) curtirostre.* 120, base of elytra and scutellum. 121, tarsal claws (without teeth). 122, apex of penis. 123, *A. (P.) lemoroi,* apex of penis (after Easton). 124–125, *A. (Aspidapion) aeneum.* 124, fore tibia of male. 125, do., female. 126–128, *A. (A.) radiolus.* 126, male fore tibia. 127, penis, ventral view. 128, do., lateral view. 129–130. *A. (A.) soror,* penis. 129, ventral view. 130, lateral view.

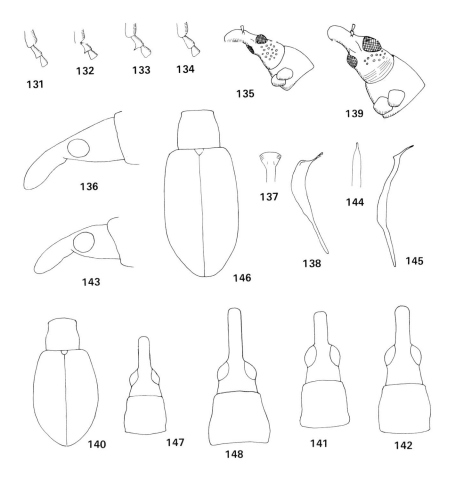

Figs 131–148. *Apion* spp. 131–134, proximal segments of male hind tarsi of *A. (Exapion)* spp. 131, *ulicis*. 132, *difficile*. 133, *fuscirostre*. 134, *genistae*. 135–138, *A.* (s.str.) *frumentarium*. 135, male temples (head in ventro-lateral view). 136, male head in profile. 137–138, penis apex (ventral) and in side view. 139–142, *A.* (s.str.) *haematodes*. 139, male temples (head in ventro-lateral view — not to scale). 140, female elytra and pronotum. 141, male head and pronotum. 142, female, do. 143–145, *A.* (s.str.) *cruentatum*. 143, male head in profile. 144–145, penis apex (ventral) and in side view. 146, *A.* (s.str.) *rubens,* female elytra and pronotum. 147–148, *A.* (s.str.) *rubiginosum*. 147, male head and pronotum. 148, female, do.

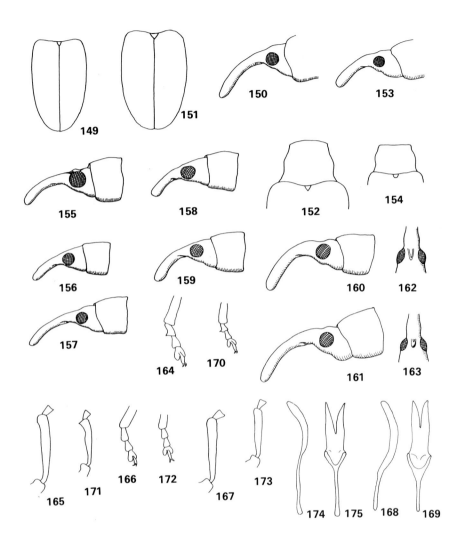

Figs 149–175. *Apion* spp. 149–150, *A. (Thymapion) cineraceum.* 149, outline of male elytra. 150, female head in profile. 151–152, *A. (T.) vicinum.* 151, outline of male elytra. 152, pronotum and base of elytra, male. 153, *A. (T.) flavimanum,* female head in profile. 154, *A. (T.) atomarium,* pronotum and base of elytra, male. 155–161, heads in profile. 155, *A. (Catapion) pubescens,* male. 156, *A. (C.) seniculus,* male 157, same, female. 158, *A. (C.) curtisii,* male. 159, same, female. 160, *A. (Taphrotopium) brunnipes,* male. 161, same, female. 162–163, male heads from above. 162, *A. (Diplapion) confluens.* 163, *A. (D.) stolidum.* 164–169, *A. (Catapion) lacertense.* 164, male hind tarsus. 165, male fore tibia. 166, female hind tarsus. 167, female fore tibia. 168, ringpiece of aedeagus, profile. 169, do., ventral view. 170–175. *A. (C.) carduorum.* 170, male hind tarsus. 171, male fore tibia. 172, female hind tarsus. 173, female fore tibia. 174, ringpiece of aedeagus, profile. 175, do., ventral view.

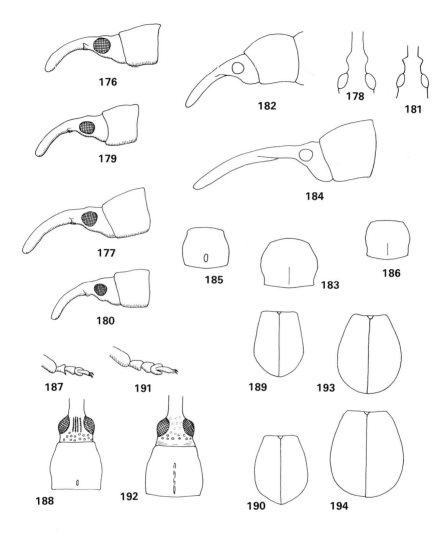

Figs 176–194. *Apion* spp. 176–178, *A. (Ceratapion) lacertense*. 176, profile of male head. 177, do., female. 178, rostral teeth of female. 179–181, *A. (C.) carduorum*. 179, profile of male head. 180, do., female. 181, rostral teeth of female. 182–183, *A. (Omphalapion) hookeri*. 182, profile of female head. 183, male pronotum. 184–185, *A. (O.) sorbi*. 184, profile of female head. 185, male pronotum. 186, *A. (O.) dispar,* male pronotum. 187–190, *A. (Pirapion) immune*. 187, male fore tarsus, showing tooth. 188, male head and pronotum. 189, outline of male elytra. 190, do., female. 191–194, *A. (P.) atratulum*. 191, male fore tarsus, unarmed. 192, male head and pronotum. 193, outline of male elytra. 194, do., female.

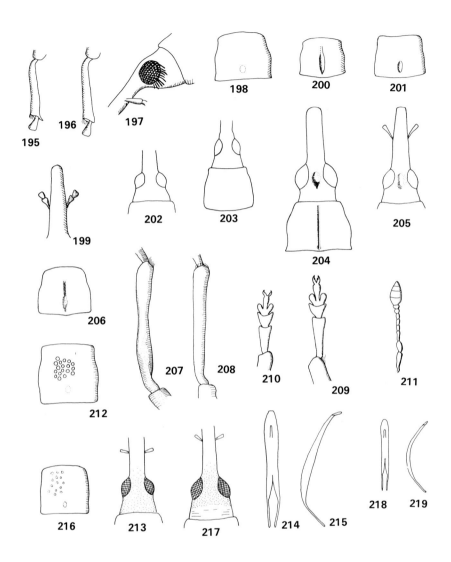

Figs 195–219. *Apion* spp. 195–197, *A. (Trichapion) simile*. 195, male hind tibia. 196, female, do. 197, female head showing setae below eye. 198–199, *A. (Pseudotrichapion) punctigerum*. 198, male pronotum. 199, female rostrum. 200, *A. (P.) astragali*, male pronotum. 201–202, *A. (P.) pisi*. 201, male pronotum. 202, female head. 203, *A. (P.) aethiops*, female head. 204–205, *A. (Eutrichapion) spencei*. 204, male head and pronotum. 205, do., female. 206, *A. (E.) ervi*, male pronotum. 207–210, *A. (E.) vorax*. 207, male fore tibia. 208, female, do. 209, male fore tarsus. 210, female, do. 211, *A. (E.) ononis*, right antenna. 212–215, *A. (E.) intermedium*. 212, female pronotum with part of puncturation. 213, female head. 214–215, penis in ventral and lateral view. 216–219, *A. (E.) tenue*. 216, female pronotum with part of puncturation. 217, female head. 218–219, penis in ventral and lateral view.

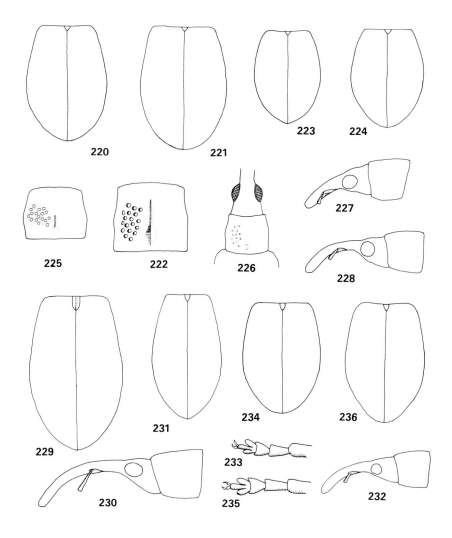

Figs 220–236. *Apion* spp. 220–222, *A. (Eutrichapion) reflexum.* 220, outline of male elytra. 221, do., female. 222, female pronotum with part of puncturation. 223–225, *A. (E.) waltoni.* 223, outline of male elytra. 224, do., female. 225, female pronotum with part of puncturation. 226–228, *A. (E.) virens.* 226, male head and pronotum with part of puncturation. 227, same, profile. 228, do., female. 229–230, *A. (E.) scutellare.* 229, outline of male elytra and scutellum. 230, female head and pronotum in profile. 231–232, *A. (E.) meliloti.* 231, outline of male elytra and scutellum. 232, female head and pronotum in profile. 233–234, *A. (E.) gyllenhali.* 233, female fore tarsus. 234, outline of elytra. 235–236, *A. (E.) afer.* 235, female fore tarsus. 236, outline of elytra.

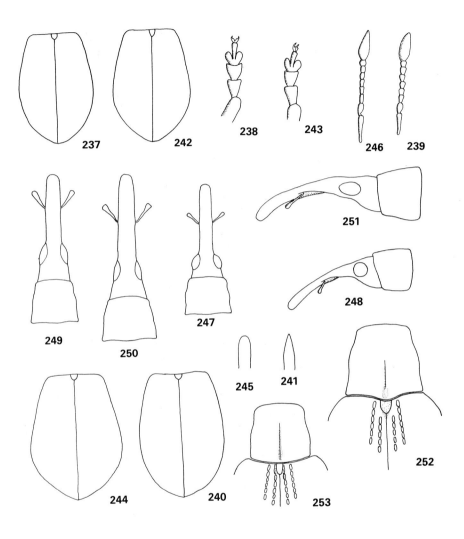

Figs 237–253. *Apion* spp. 237–241, *A. (Eutrichapion) loti.* 237, outline of female elytra. 238, female fore tarsus. 239, female antenna. 240, outline of male elytra. 241, apex of penis. 242–245, *A. (E.) modestum.* 242, outline of female elytra. 243, female fore tarsus. 244, outline of male elytra. 245, apex of penis. 246–248, *A. (E.) afer.* 246, female antenna. 247, outline of female head and pronotum from above. 248, same, profile. 249–251, *A. (E.) gyllenhali.* 249, outline of male head and pronotum from above. 250, do., female. 251, do., female, in profile. 252, *A. (Oxystoma) pomonae,* male pronotum and base of elytra. 253, *A. (O.) subulatum,* female pronotum and base of elytra.

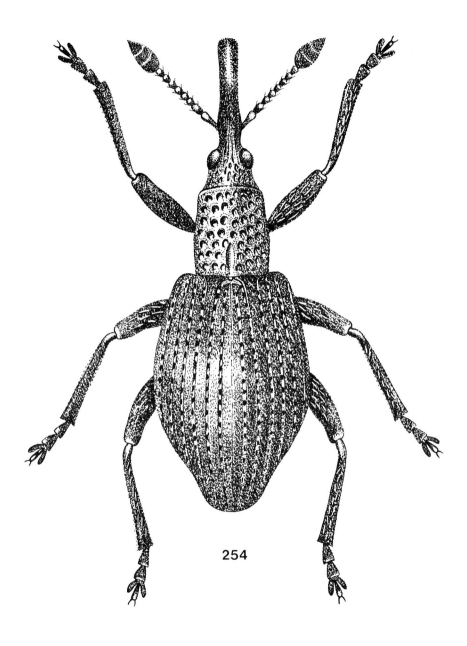

Fig. 254. *Apion onopordi*, male.

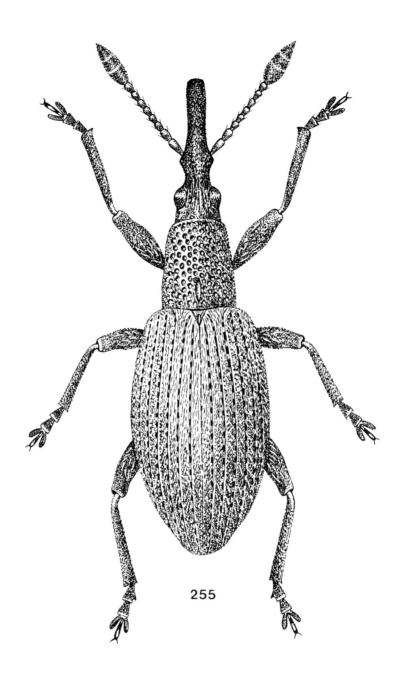

255

Fig. 255. *Apion carduorum*, male.

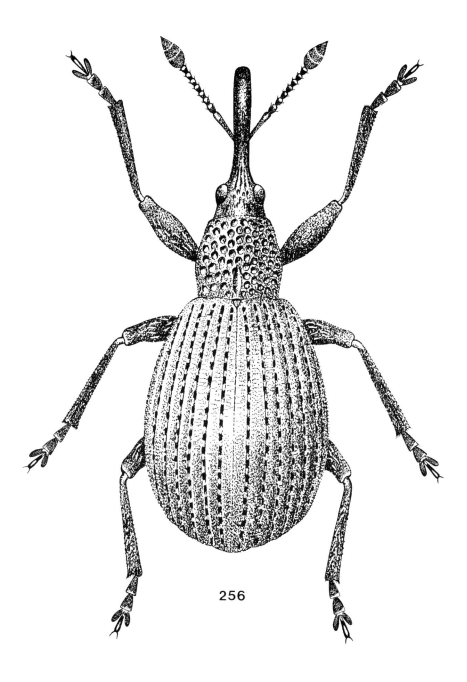

256

Fig. 256. *Apion atratulum,* male.

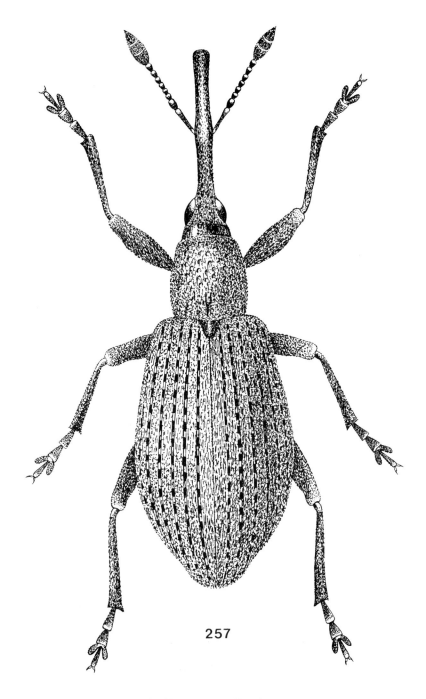

257

Fig. 257. *Apion scutellare*, female.

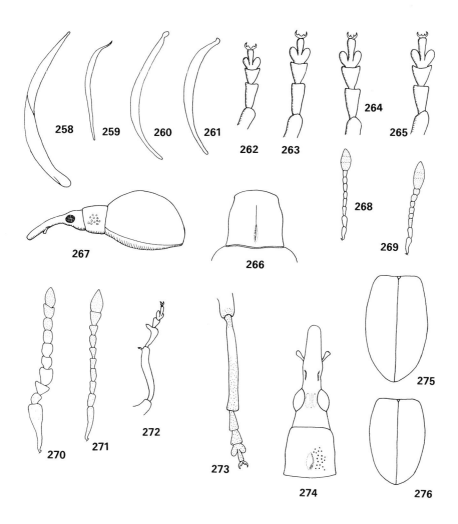

Figs 258–276. *Apion* spp. 258–261, *A. (Oxystoma)* spp., penes in side view. 258, *pomonae*. 259, *craccae*. 260, *subulatum*. 261, *cerdo*. 262–265, *A. (Oxystoma)* spp., fore tarsi. 262, male *subulatum*. 263, female *subulatum*. 264, male *cerdo*. 265, female *cerdo*. 266, *A. (O.) cerdo*, female pronotum. 267, *A. (Protapion) filirostre*, profile with part of puncturation of pronotum. 268, *A. (P.) nigritarse*, female antenna. 269, *A. (P.) dichroum*, female antenna. 270–272, *A. (P.) difforme*. 270, male antenna. 271, female antenna. 272, male fore tibia and tarsus. 273–274, *A. (P.) laevicolle*. 273, male hind tibia and tarsus. 274, male head and pronotum, including part of puncturation. 275, *A. (P.) varipes*, outline of female elytra. 276, *A. (P.) dissimile*, outline of female elytra.

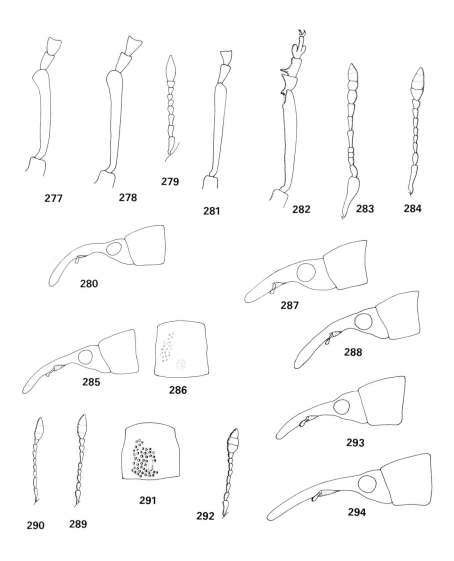

Figs 277–294. *Apion (Protapion)* spp. 277–280, *A. (P.) varipes*. 277, male fore tibia. 278, do., female. 279, female antenna. 280, female head and pronotum in profile. 281–285, *A. (P.) dissimile*. 281, female fore tibia. 282, male fore tibia and tarsus. 283, male antenna. 284, female antenna. 285, female head and pronotum in profile. 286–290, *A. (P.) schoenherri*. 286, male pronotum from above, with part of puncturation. 287, male head and pronotum in profile. 288, do., female. 289, male antenna. 290, female antenna. 291–294, *A. (P.) trifolii*. 291, male pronotum with part of puncturation. 292, male antenna. 293, male head and pronotum in profile. 294, female, do.

98

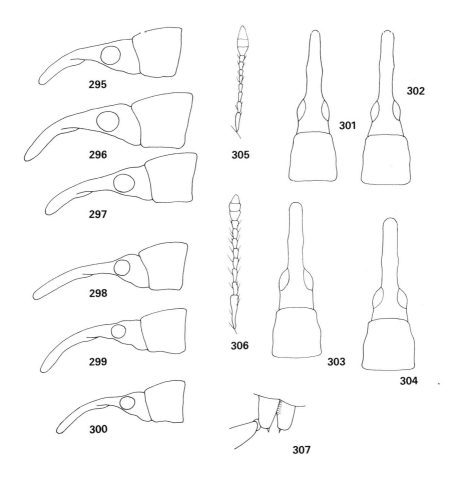

Figs 295–307. *Apion (Protapion)* spp. 295–300, heads in profile (not to scale). 295, male *assimile*. 296, male *ononicola*. 297, male *apricans*. 298, female *apricans*. 299, female *ononicola*. 300, female *assimile*. 301–304, heads from above (not to scale). 301, male *ononicola*. 302, male *apricans*. 303, male *assimile*. 304, male *ryei*. 305, *A. (P.) assimile,* male antenna. 306–307, *A. (P.) ononicola*. 306, male antenna. 307, male fore coxae from the front, left trochanter and femur removed.

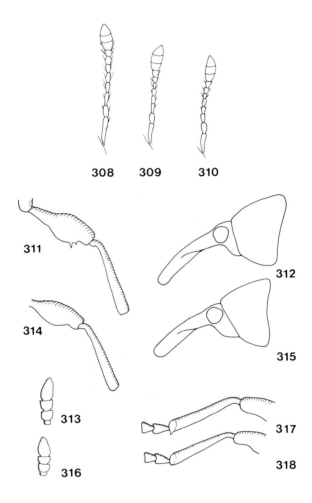

Figs 308–318. *Apion* and *Nanophyes* spp. 308–310, antennae of *A. (Protapion)* spp. 308, female *ononicola*. 309, female *assimile*. 310, female *ryei*. 311–313, *N. gracilis*. 311, female femur and tibia. 312, female head and pronotum in profile. 313, female antennal club. 314–318, *N. marmoratus*. 314, female femur and tibia. 315, female head and pronotum in profile. 316, female antennal club. 317, male hind tibia. 318, female, do.

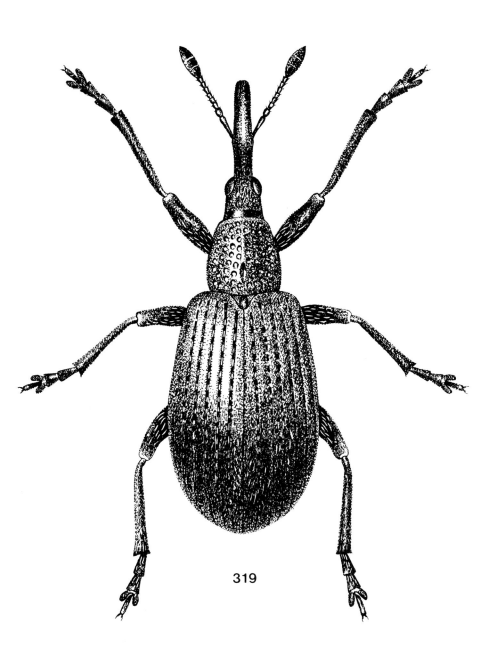

319

Fig. 319. *Apion loti,* male.

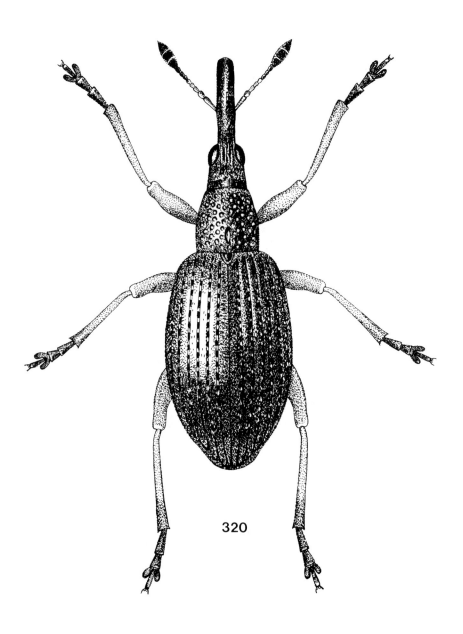

Fig. 320. *Apion dichroum,* female.

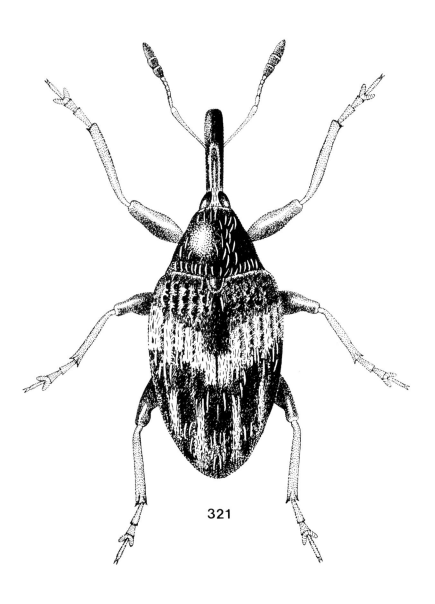

Fig. 321. *Nanophyes marmoratus,* male.

Index

Synonyms, and page references to figures, are in italics.

sheppardi (Choragus) 12, 17, 25, *72*
shrubs 6
sicardi (Eutrichapion) 20
sieving 7
simile (Trichapion) 11, 19, 51, *90*
sodium hydroxide 9
sorbi (Omphalapion) 11, 13, 19, 49, *89*
soror (Aspidapion) 11, 18, 40, *86*
spencii (Eutrichapion) 15, 20, 53, *90*
spermatheca 9
sterna 10
stolidum (Diplapion) 12, 19, 46, *88*
storeboxes 8
striatum (Pirapion) 19, 50
subfossils 7
subulatum (Oxystoma) 12, 20, 59, *84, 92, 97*
sweep net 7
Synapion 19, 35, 49

Taeniapion 18, 35, 40, 51
Taphrotopium 19, 35, 47
Tenthredinidae 51
tenue (Eutrichapion) 13, 20, 53, *90*
Thymapion 18, 35, 44, 51
tomentosus (Pselaphorhynchites) 13, 14, 17, 29, *78*
trees 6
Trichapion 19, 36, 51

trifolli (Protapion) 15, 20, 62, *98*
Tropideres 16, 23
Tropideres (subgen.) 16

ulicis (Exapion) 7, 15, 18, 42, *82, 84, 87*
uncinatus (Pselaphorhynchites) 17
unicolor (Eutrichapion) 19   '
Urodon 17, 25
Urodoninae 25
Urodontidae 4, 5, 17, 21, 25
urticarium (Taeniapion) 15, 18, 41

vacuum net 7
variegatus (Anthribus) 16
varipes (Protapion) 15, 20, 61, *97, 98*
varius (Anthribus) 16
ventrites 10
viciae (Eutrichapion) 15, 20, 53
vicinum (Thymapion) 13, 19, 45, *85, 88*
Vincenzellus 10
violaceum (Perapion) 14, 18, 37, *85, 86*
virens (Eutrichapion) 14, 15, 20, 56, *91*
vorax (Eutrichapion) 7, 15, 20, 54, *90*

Wales 7
waltoni (Eutrichapion) 12, 20, 55, *91*
Watsonian vice counties 7
Worcester 7